SECRETS OF
MODERN WITCHCRAFT
REVEALED

SECRETS OF MODERN WITCHCRAFT REVEALED

Unlocking the Mysteries of the Magickal Arts

LADY SABRINA

High Priestess and Founder
of Our Lady of Enchantment
Seminary of Wicca

A Citadel Press Book
Published by Carol Publishing Group

Carol Publishing Group edition, 1999

A Citadel Press Book
Published by Carol Publishing Group
Citadel Press is a registered trademark of Carol Communications, Inc.

Editorial, sales and distribution, rights and permissions inquiries should be addressed to
Carol Publishing Group, 120 Enterprise Avenue, Secaucus, N.J. 07094

In Canada: Canadian Manda Group, One Atlantic Avenue, Suite 105, Toronto, Ontario
M6K 3E7

Carol Publishing Group books may be purchased in bulk at special discounts for sales
promotion, fund-raising, or educational purposes. Special editions can be
created to specifications. For details, contact Special Sales Department,
Carol Publishing Group, 120 Enterprise Avenue, Secaucus, N.J. 07094.

Manufactured in the United States of America
10 9 8 7 6 5 4 3 2

Library of Congress Cataloging-in-Publication Data

Sabrina, Lady.
    Secrets of modern witchcraft revealed : unlocking the mysteries of
the magickal arts / Lady Sabrina.
        p.   cm.
    "A Citadel Press book."
    Includes bibliographical references and index.
    ISBN 0-8065-2017-5 (pbk.)
    1. Witchcraft.   I. Title.
BF1571.S225   1998
133.4'3--dc21   98-28931
                                                        CIP

To all the members of Our Lady of Enchantment, especially those who have given their time and energy to this book. Thank you, Aristaeus, Autumn, Balaam, Cassius, Damaclease, Galadriel, and most of all, Mike Lewis, for being patient and understanding.

CONTENTS

INTRODUCTION

Handed down from generation to generation, Witchcraft has a rich and powerful history—a history which, told and retold through the ages, has been tainted by exaggeration and twisted by falsehood. So why has Witchcraft persisted in spite of centuries of misunderstanding and persecution? Perhaps because it draws upon a sixth sense, an undeniable instinct buried deep within the heart of humanity. Whatever the reason, witchcraft obviously satisfies some basic need or it would not have survived.

The earliest Witches were leaders of their communities. They dealt with its basic concerns: birth, life, death, the welfare of the tribe, and the success of its warriors. By all accounts, they were able to manipulate the natural world using supernatural abilities. They were focused, had an eye for the subtle differences in nature, and had a deep sense of the rhythmic vibrations which connect all living things. They were "naturalists" in the extreme.

Witches were the first ecologists. They understood the need for humanity to live in balance with nature, and the force that they perceived maintained it. Much of their magick was (and still is) directed to this end. They observed the seasons, their friends, animals, and the effects nature had on all of them. They watched the night sky and noted the influence of the sun, moon, and stars. Nothing escaped the ever-watchful eye of the Witch.

The pursuance of Witchcraft is not much different now than it was for our ancestors. It is usually the strong need or desire for something like love, good health, or economic security that sets one upon the path of discovery. When time is of the essence, and conventional methods fail, even the most skeptical will turn to the magickal arts for aid and comfort.

Witchcraft is not complicated. It is not without structural reason, nor is it in opposition to nature. In fact, it is just the opposite. Witchcraft teaches us that by aligning ourselves with the natural flow of the universe, through reasonable methods, we can simply and effortlessly get what we need and want. All it really takes is some imagination, desire, and a willingness to consider what most people don't understand.

For those who are seeking, or just discovering, alternative spirituality, I assure you that Witchcraft is not evil. At least not any more than lighting a votive candle, praying for a sick friend, or carrying a lucky charm is. However, there are some who do view Witchcraft as evil. This is only because organized religion (primarily the Christian church) has conditioned them to fear anything which strays from their narrow condemning view. After all, if you have the ability to fend for yourself, solve your own problems, and choose your own method of spiritual expression, why would you need the confined structure of a church?

Witchcraft, like any science or philosophical system, must be approached from a liberal point of view. When looked at objectively, we see that Witchcraft is just another theoretical body of knowledge. It is a process, not a person. Therefore it is *neutral*, incapable of being either good or evil. Like all belief systems, Witchcraft is only as good or evil as the people using it.

So, what are Witches really like? Well, for one thing, they are not ugly old hags or offensive lechers. The very idea of this is ludicrous. If a Witch has, as it is believed, special powers, then she or he must be able to project the illusion of beauty and success, if not actually attain it. When one has the ability to manipulate the forces of nature, it only follows that one has the power to create an aura of charm and well-being.

While the ideal way to learn Witchcraft, or any of the magickal arts, is to become apprenticed to a seasoned practitioner, a great deal can be learned on one's own. Some of the greatest musicians and artists had little or no formal training, but by having a gift and being willing to work, they became masters of their craft. The same is true for Witchcraft.

Witchcraft, when properly practiced, offers many benefits. When done with friends or within the confines of a coven, it provides an outlet for the human need of ritual. Contemporary life being the way it is allows most of us very little kinship with the earth. We tend to overlook the changing of the seasons, important passages of life, and the existence of other living creatures. Witchcraft helps us reconnect with the forces of the universe and reclaim our spiritual identity. When this happens, personal power is restored and we become truly happy and content.

To become a Witch, you must first learn to love yourself. You must put your goals and desires first. You have to become completely involved with what you want, or you won't get it. You don't see anyone succeed by allowing every little thing, annoying person, or indulgence to interrupt their concentration. You've got to be obsessed with what you want and work for it all the time. You can't be a part-time Witch and hope to achieve full-time success.

Witchcraft, magick, and all of the occult sciences are meant to help people, including yourself. The presumptuous notion that you shouldn't use magick for personal gain, but only to help others, is pure foolishness propagated by the ignorant, and it bears no historical relevance. If you study the lives of famous Witches and magicians, you will find that they lived well and enjoyed the creature comforts of their time.

One final note about Witchcraft and magick: they take physical time and effort to make work. There is no point in performing a complex ritual to get a new car if you aren't willing to even go look for one; participation is the key to being an effective Witch. You must initiate the activity on the physical plane and then nourish it on the astral one. The powers-that-be will always assist you, but only when you have made the effort to deal with your physical situation. So don't bother to do that love spell on the person next door if you are too shy to even speak with him. When all is said and done, if all that was required to manifest desire was, say, merely lighting a candle, there would be no poverty, suffering, or death.

Part I

The Elements of Modern Witchcraft

1

Witchcraft and Magick

Magic is no great mystery, save to those who have never investigated or practiced it. It's the natural process of moving energy from within ourselves (or within natural objects) to create a positive change.

—Scott Cunningham and David Harrington, *Spell Crafts*

Among those who practice Witchcraft and the magickal arts, it is commonly held that each thought, idea, or action sets up a vibration on the Astral Plane.[1] Not only are our thoughts and ideas there, but also present are exact duplicates of every object and living thing on earth. When the Witch sends out a powerful thought-form,[2]

[1]Astral (Latin *astar*, "star") refers to the level of awareness in the etheric world that is close to the mundane world; a vibration faster than the earth's vibration but looks similar to the earth's when one perceives it clairvoyantly.

[2]Thought-forms are different shapes of ethereal substance, defined or cloudy, large or small, varying in color and density, that float through space or hover over people's heads. They are capable of being perceived clairvoyantly; ergs of energy emanating from the head area are charged with degrees of intelligence and emotion, and occupy their position in space according to their disposition.

such as those used in spells and enchantments, a vibration is created on the Astral Plane. This vibration is actually a wave of energy which seeks out and impresses the counterpart of the person, place, or thing on which the spell has been cast. Once the astral counterpart has been touched, then its earthly identical twin (person, place, or thing) responds accordingly.

In order to create a thought-form powerful enough to produce a reaction on the Astral Plane, the Witch must be totally focused. He or she must have a crystal-clear picture of the intended target in their mind, and the desired outcome. Once the image of desire is absolutely clear, the practitioner must then generate enough energy to actually turn it into a thought-form. When the thought-form and the intended objective meet, manifestation of desire is realized.

Essentially, magick is the art and science of causing change to occur in accordance with will. It is the process which allows the practitioner to create bigger and better thought-forms, which in turn replace impractical or dysfunctional thought-forms. Once created, a thought-form works like an invisible magick wand, and changes or modifies targeted destinations at the discretion of its creator.

In order to create the perfect thought-form, which will magickally transform your life, you must be able to attain the right emotional state, and frame of mind. You need to get into a state of mind where you are able to suspend disbelief in the primitive actions of the magickal process itself so the higher (superconscious) self can move and work uninhibited by the conditioned,[3] practical (conscious) self.

The magickal process is really quite simple when you look at it from a logical point of view. The comparison between magick and a Broadway play is a good example. In the play, like in a

---

[3]Conditioned self: the part of the mind or way of thinking which has been pre-programmed and trained by an outside influence or authority figure.

magickal rite, you are the actor. As the actor, you are going to say certain things and perform certain actions within specific scenes or segments of the rite. Though the play may be total fantasy, it is none the less real during the performance. The only difference between a Broadway play and a magickal rite is the audience. The Broadway play is produced for real people, and the magickal rite is acted out for the benefit of the truly conscious mind, or higher self.

If you are a good actor and play your part well, you will be convincing no matter how far-fetched the script is. Magick is the same. If you can act out your desire with enough energy and conviction, you will engross the conscious mind to the point where it becomes distracted from disbelief. And once the self, or conscious mind, is distracted from mundane reality, the higher mind, or truly conscious self, is able to raise its paranormal powers to the proper level of creation. Once this happens, the higher self is in a position to manifest the image of desire.

Think about the possibilities! Consider how the Broadway production, with its elaborate sets, beautiful costumes, and enchanting music, has the ability to sweep you off your feet through pure illusion. This is exactly what a magickal rite does. It distracts your attention from the reality of conditioned thinking. For it is during the moment of distraction that the higher self is able to focus its full power on the creation of the thought-form, and thereby manifest desire.

Magick, as an art or science, offers an extensive library of study. And just like the arts and sciences, magick provides its practitioners with a variety of options. The highly trained and sophisticated adherent will most likely lean toward ceremonial magick. Those who appreciate structure, but without its complications, will find ritual magick very satisfying. For the occasional practitioner who favors spell-crafting and natural magick, Witchcraft will be the first choice.

Magickal Concepts

The arts of Witchcraft and magick have some very definable concepts which explain why and how they work. These concepts are, in reality, principles which are considered to be the basic substance, or laws, from which all magickal works are derived. These laws are the Law of Similarity and the Law of Contact or Contagion, both of which come under the single designation of Sympathetic Magick. And, for the most part, Sympathetic Magick is the very heart and soul of Witchcraft.

The first principle of magick is the Law of Similarity. This law is also referred to as homeopathic, or imitative, magick. It basically states that like produces like, or that an effect may resemble its cause. Simply put, whatever you do to the symbolic representation of a person, place, or thing will directly affect that same person, place, or thing. This all goes back to the idea of everything having an astral counterpart, which can be influenced by magickally created thought-forms.

A good example of Sympathetic Magick is the voodoo doll. The Witch or magician fashions a doll to look like the individual  they wish to influence. Then, depending on the circumstances, the Witch will proceed to heal or hurt their targeted victim through magickal conjurations. Because the doll looks like (imitates) the intended victim, it is capable of creating a link with the individual's astral counterpart, or twin. Therefore, what is done to the doll will traverse the link and affect what lies at the other end.

In partnership with the Law of Similarity is a second principle, the Law of Contact or Contagion, often referred to as Contagious Magick. This law states that things which have been in contact with each other will continue to act on each other, even at a distance, after all physical contact has been broken.

Because of this, it is possible to use a person's picture, article of clothing, or even their handwriting as a magickal link. These links are often referred to as tag-locks, or relics, and are of primary importance in certain spells and enchantments, especially where love and friendship are concerned.

It is interesting to note that Homeopathic Magick and Contagious Magick can be worked separately or in combination. When used in conjunction with each other, they create a powerful dominating effect. This ability to dominate is the main reason why some practitioners of voodoo, as well as other magickal sects, use clothing, hair, and nails from their victims when making a doll, because the more things the doll has in common with its counterpart, the better. This is particularly true if the spell being cast involves love and passion, or anything which involves the emotions. When emotions are involved, it usually doesn't take take too much to sway the victim one way or the other. At least this seems to be the case when the practitioner is very powerful and focused in intent.

Working With Magick

Understanding how magick works and actually making it work are two different things. Everyone has a pretty good idea of what goes into the making of a Broadway play, but stand the average person on an empty stage with a crate of costumes, say "Go for it," and see what happens. In nine out of ten cases the individual will find himself or herself totally lost and bewildered. Suddenly, faced with the physical reality of *doing*, rather than just *imagining*, it becomes very frightening. This is especially true if an individual does not possess the proper skills for the job at hand.

Magick, like the production of a play, is a challenge, a challenge which must be approached through knowledge, experience, and the comprehension of proper procedure. Magick also requires skill and planning, as well as an understanding of some very unique concepts. Similar to the production of a play, once you know how to go about it, the only thing standing in your way is the actual doing of it.

In addition to the laws of magick, there are some significant underlying principles which enhance as well as lend credence to its overall body of working knowledge. When viewed objectively, these principles, or basic tenets, are nothing more than good-old common sense. They are referred to by some as the powers of the magus, by others as the four cornerstones of magick, and by Witches as the Witch's pyramid. Simply put, they are rules of thumb for the Witch and magician to follow, and are expressed in the ability to know, to will, to dare, and to keep silent.

To Know

This means knowledge about what you are doing. You can't produce a play if you don't know the difference between the orchestra pit and center stage. You can't do magick if you do not understand, or know, the difference between its basic working principles and how to use its fundamental concepts. You need to know what you are doing and why. Knowledge is power.

To Will

This is the ability to concentrate, focus your attention, and will your personal energy sources to do what you want them to do. You must be able to force your will upon the universe in a positive and powerful way if you are going to accomplish your goal. Just like the producer of a play, you must be able to control your surroundings and will others to do as you deem necessary.

To Dare

This is the courage to challenge yourself and your ideas. You must be able to stand up for your beliefs and demand your rights. You must dare to have the courage to make your will manifest what you desire, and you must do this without fear or doubt. You must be able to command respect from your peers, as well as from the forces with which you will be working. You must dare to be strong.

To Keep Silent

By far the hardest of the four rules. To keep silent means just that. It is the ability to turn off that voice in your head which chatters incessantly, and I might add, needlessly. You must shut out, and off, all outside distractions and go inward. You must learn to concentrate and focus. Silence also has a partner—the mouth. You must learn to keep it shut and not crow about every little piece of work you do. Every time you speak of your magickal works you dissipate their energy and power. You must learn to be and keep silent.

Along with the four cornerstones of magick come four auxiliary considerations, or rules. These additional concepts are the rules of the road for smart Witches and magicians. They provide the guidelines for all magickal rites and spells. By using these rules you will be able to structure and organize your magickal operations effectively. These concepts include proper necessity, proper elements, proper planning, and proper energy.

Proper Necessity

What is it that you want? Do you really need what you are lusting after? How emotionally involved with desire are you? What are you willing to do to get it?

It is difficult to build energy and power without passionate drive. You must have the emotional drive equivalent to the survival instinct if you are going to activate those energy levels of your mind which produce the thought-forms, which create change. Wanting is not enough. Everyone wants things. The reason most magick spells don't work is because the individual doesn't really need what it is that he or she thinks they need.

Because of this, the level of energy needed to make the spell work isn't readily available.

Proper Elements

To make any magickal operation work you must have the required elements. The elements are the physical props, tools, and corresponding symbols which link you to your objective. This means that if you are doing a spell which calls for a red candle, rose incense, and a heart-shaped box, you must have a red candle, rose incense, and a heart-shaped box to make the spell work. If you only have two of the three items called for, you will not get the results specified for using all three things. Remember, magick works by creating an illusion which distracts the conscious mind. The illusion is usually created by using elemental tools and special symbolic objects. To make any spell or magickal operation work, you must have all of the physical elements called for.

Proper Planning

It is important to plan your magickal works and spells ahead of time, just as you would plan to produce a Broadway play. You don't just get up one morning and say "Hey, I think I'll get the gang together and put on a play this evening," and then go out and order tickets, posters, and advertising before talking with the gang and planning everything out.

Magick and spell-crafting are no different. You need to plan your works ahead of time. There will be some works which will need to coincide with certain phases of the moon, or planetary energies. There will be places and times which will be more conducive to your work than others. All the details must be carefully thought out and planned in advance. The appropriate symbols, tools, and even music must be considered. Planning is a necessity if your magickal spells are going to work.

Proper Energy

This is the personal power you will project into your goal. The need—as in necessity—must be present. You must desire. You must be totally, even lustfully, involved with your goal. This involvement is mandatory if you are going to be able to raise the level of energy needed to manifest the thought-form, which in turn will accomplish your desire.

One hundred percent of your attention, emotion, and energy must be given at the moment of conception when you force your intent out and into the atmosphere. It is your personal power and energy which makes the spell work. You can have all the right ingredients, but if the energy and enthusiasm are not there the magick will not work. Your spell will be just as flat and ineffectual as a play with indifferent actors. Energy is what gives animation to life.

Thoughts and Ideas

Magick is an art; it is a science; it is your ability to make changes in your life according to your own will. Magick, whether an elaborate ceremony or a simple candle spell, allows you to move and bend reality. It is through the movement of energy that you will manipulate the forces around you and magickally recreate your universe. Magick is high-powered, positive thinking with booster rockets. It gives you the upper hand and edge in life. It allows you to be anything you want to be, and gives you the power to help yourself as well as others.

Magick is a marvelous tool which can be used to enhance your life. It is not a substitute for reality or hard work, and won't suddenly transform a sow's ear into a silk purse. However magick can, and will, provide you with the options and tools you need to make manifest your highest ideals.

A simple candle spell, an enchantment spoken under the full moon, or a common herbal charm all have the power and

potential to make your wishes come true. With careful attention
to detail, moderate self-control, and a true inner desire to make
something happen, anyone can wave their magick wand with
assured success. The key is to know what you want, dare to meet
the challenge, and discreetly keep silent as you will your desire
into being.

2

Mind Over Matter

Meditation is an activity of mental consciousness. It involves one part of the mind observing, analyzing, and dealing with the rest of the mind.

—Kathleen McDonald, *How to Meditate*

Meditation is something everyone can do. It is not complicated or restricted to the jurisdiction of any specific Wiccan or magickal tradition. It is simply the best method for clearing away the negative thoughts and vibrations which interfere with the magickal abilities of the individual.

Essentially, meditation is the ability to observe and understand individual reality. Its ultimate aim is to awaken that subtle level of consciousness which resides deep within the human mind. Once this area of consciousness has been tapped into, extraordinary things begin to happen. The individual begins to see things as they really are, rather than as he or she has been told they should be.

Meditation is the process through which you learn to become totally honest with yourself. It allows you to take a good look at who you really are and see what areas you need to work on. Once you are in touch with your inner feelings and higher self, you begin to grow and progress both physically and spiritually.

Besides being a good method of self-analysis, meditation also teaches you how to control your mind. Control is important because the mind is not a physical thing that *has* thoughts and feelings; it *is* thoughts and feelings. Therefore, what you program into your mind is what it becomes. In order for you to accomplish anything on a magickal or spiritual level, you must be in complete control of your entire being, and this includes your mind.

Unfortunately, the mind has the tendency to behave like a spoiled child, doing what it wants when it wants. Then if you attempt to force it into some radically different pattern of behavior, it rebels. It rebels by blocking your concentration with useless information and endless chatter, keeping you distracted and therefore unable to achieve your goal. Meditation provides you with the behavioral skills to teach this unruly child manners and discipline.

Meditation has long been a popular pasttime among those interested in metaphysics. Because of this, there are a variety of methods and styles to choose from. You can lie on the couch doing TM, relax in a chair practicing Quiet Attentiveness, or sit twisted up like a pretzel while performing Zen. Method and position are a matter of personal choice; no one arrangement is better than the other. They all have the same dual purpose— physical relaxation and mind control.

As you can see, there are a variety of meditation techniques, styles, and physical positions. However, there are only two types of meditation: stabilized meditation and analytical meditation.

Stabilized Meditation

Stabilized meditation is used to train the body and mind to be still. It is usually expressed as single-point concentration, and is a prerequisite for analytical meditation and any type of lasting insight. The aim of stabilized meditation is to help the body relax and reach a level of poised confidence. Once the body is relaxed through controlled breathing and concentration, the mind is trained to visualize an image or concept without interruption.

Unfortunately, concentration without interruption is difficult to achieve because it is not a normal state of mind. Stop for just a moment and try to concentrate on one thing. It is just about impossible, because all of a sudden the mind starts running amuck, jumping from one thing to another: a sound outside, the temperature of the room, thoughts of what you will do later, or how hungry you are. It thinks about everything except the one thing you want it to. The mind is a busy spoiled child and does not like being interrupted, let alone told what to do.

When it comes to magick and Witchcraft, all this internal chatter causes confusion and prevents concentration. In order for magick to work, the Witch or magician must be able to concentrate on a single objective without any distraction. The mind must be brought under control if you are going to succeed.

Stabilized meditation is hard work. It takes time and effort to produce results. But with patience and persistence it can be done and become a valuable asset. Just like the unruly child, once the mind has been taught some manners, it becomes a delight to work with rather than a disappointment or a burden.

Analytical Meditation

Analytical meditation is crucial to the development of the intelligent, creative, and conceptual side of the personality. It is a standard of contemplation which helps to develop clarity of thought and define desire. When it is used in conjunction with stabilized meditation, it brings direct and intuitive knowing.

Analytical meditation helps to clear away the debris left behind by our conditioned thinking. It helps eliminate those ideas, thoughts, and feelings that cause personal and emotional harm. Then, once the negative thoughts and feelings are gone, they can be replaced with happy, positive ones of our own making.

The process is very simple. Once you have stabilized the mind and body, you can then begin to analyze what is wrong with it. Just like a screaming and ranting child, once you have calmed it down you can then reason with it and discover the problem. Until there is quiet, all you have is confusion and chaos.

Stabilized and analytical meditation work together. They are partners, just as parents are. The father, stabilized meditation, quiets the turbulent storm so the mother, analytical meditation, can reason out what the problem is and then solve it.

Working With Meditation

Meditation is good exercise for the mind, and just like any exercise, the more you do it, the better at it you become. I suggest you set aside fifteen minutes a day for your meditation practices. Try not to let days and weeks go by without meditating. If you do, just as with physical exercise, you will fall out of practice and find it very difficult the next time you try to do it. The mind is very much like the body in its need for exercise; the more you work with it during meditation, the healthier and happier it becomes.

When it comes to meditation, the very first thing to consider is where you will do it. This need not turn into a project or family feud. Basically, you can meditate just about anytime and anyplace. All you really need is an area where you can be alone for fifteen minutes. If this poses a problem, just tell the spouse and kids you are going to clean the basement. I guarantee that no one will ask to accompany you!

When it comes to selecting a site for meditation, solitude is the priority. The area you choose must be free from noises such as traffic, TV, radio, and children at play. It should be well ventilated and large enough for you to sit or lie comfortably. This basically rules out the bedroom closet or crawl space under the house. Don't laugh—I know people who have scrunched themselves up in the back of the closet only to be embarrassed by their mate looking for a change of clothes.

Meditation is good for the mind and body. It gives you time to recharge your batteries and put things into perspective. Everyone can find fifteen minutes a day to meditate if they really want to. But for those of you who regard regular meditation as "mission impossible," here are some helpful hints:

- Get up one-half hour earlier in the morning, before other family members. By doing this, you can pretty much choose any space you want for your meditation without interference.

- Busy mothers with small children can take advantage of their young ones' nap time and meditate during that time. Take the phone off the hook; turn off the TV and close the drapes. Spend some quality time finding out who you are and what you want.

- There is nothing quite like a good, hot bath to relax the physical body. Use your bath time as your meditation time. You will be left alone and have the entire room to yourself. Just be sure to lock the door behind you.

- Take advantage of your lunch hour. Get into your car and drive to some quiet place with a nice view. This will be relaxing and provide you with a perfect meditation setup. You can sit comfortably in your car during any type of weather, safe and secure from natural or imposed interference.

- In the evening when the family gathers around the TV or computer, ask to be excused for fifteen minutes. Tell everyone you need some quiet time for yourself. Pretty soon everyone will be used to mommy or daddy going to the bedroom after dinner for quiet time.

Basic Meditation

Meditation is not a complicated process, nor is it physically demanding. Once you have mastered the technique for quieting the mind, you will be able to do it just about anytime or any-place. The following exercise will introduce you to the world of meditation; it will also begin the process of relaxing the body in preparation for focused contemplation. For this exercise you will need a small kitchen timer and some soothing New Age music.[1]

Relaxation Exercise

Put on some soothing New Age music. Get yourself comfortable and begin to relax. Begin at the top of the head and work downward.

Tilt your head forward, backward, and then from side to side, breathing deeply three times each. Relax.

Continue down through the neck, chest, back, arms, and abdomen, breathing deeply three times for each body section. Relax.

Then continue on down through the thighs, knees, ankles, feet, and toes. Check all muscles you can feel and be sure that they are relaxed. If your breathing is even and calm, relaxation will come quickly and easily.

As you direct your breathing, exclude all thoughts and sensations and fix your consciousness totally on the breathing process.

Follow the air as it enters and leaves your nostrils and lungs. Become acutely aware of the rhythm of inhalation and exhala-

[1] There are many New Age tapes created especially for meditation. These tapes are designed to help calm and relax both the body and mind with sounds of nature. "Entrance to the Secret Lagoon," "Crystal Cave (Back to Atlantis)," and "Upper Astral Suite" by Upper Astral are some good examples of mood-altering meditation music. Upper Astral can be reached at Valley of the Sun, Box 38, Malibu, CA 90265.

tion. Whenever this awareness is interrupted by a thought or sound, dismiss it and return your attention to breathing. As often as you are distracted, you must return your attention to breathing.

Continue observing your breath for approximately one minute, just long enough to withdraw and quiet your mind and senses. Depending on the rhythm of your respiration, you will perform nine to fifteen inhalations and exhalations during the one-minute period.

Upon completion of this technique, proceed with the following meditation practice.

Basic Meditation Exercise

Step One: Place a single flower in a plain white or black vase. Set this in front of you so you can easily see it, but place it a comfortable distance away so there will be no eyestrain involved.

Step Two: Relax and perform your breathing exercise as previously discussed. Repeat this for about three minutes.

Step Three: Now that you are completely relaxed, begin to become involved with the flower to the extent that none of the other senses (and no thought) will distract you. Take your time to visually examine the flower's structure, form, texture, and color. Behold the flower's beauty and detail.

If you notice your attention has wandered, gently but firmly bring your mind back to the flower and continue your examination. As often as your mind wanders, return to the flower. By forcing your mind to concentrate on what you want it to do, you will eventually be able to bring it under control.

The entire purpose of this meditation is to teach the mind how to concentrate on what you want it to, rather than running here and there and dissipating your energy. In time, you will be able to focus your attention directly on any given situation, thus enabling you to make quick and accurate decisions.

The Guardian Spirit

It has long been believed that at birth each individual is given a guardian spirit. This spirit is a form of ethereal intelligence which lives on the Astral Plane and communicates directly with its individual ward. The countenance the guardian spirit takes on greatly depends on the culture and religion into which the individual is born. For example, in African society the guardian spirit is believed to be a beloved ancestor. In most Western Christian cultures, the spirit guide is perceived as a guardian angel. In some Native American tribes, totem animals are believed to be the guardians. No matter what form this spirit takes, its job is still the same: that of protector and defender.

Learning to identify and work with your guardian spirit can be very profitable. This is because your guardian spirit resides mainly on the Astral Plane, and is privy to information well before you are. It sees and knows what has happened to you in the past, and is well aware of what the future holds. By contacting your guardian spirit, you are able to tap into its vast reservoir of personal knowledge.

The following meditation exercise is designed to help you contact your guardian spirit. To do it, you will need your kitchen timer, a notebook, a pen, sea salt, a compass, a white candle, and a meditation robe.[2]

Spirit Guide Meditation Exercise

The first couple of times you do this exercise, choose a place where you can be alone for at least fifteen minutes, dim the lights, and turn off all outside distractions, including the TV, radio, and stereo.

---

[2] A meditation robe can be any loose-fitting robelike garment. A white cotton bathrobe, which is used for no other purpose, works best. It is a good idea to keep clothing used for ritual and magickal practices separate from clothes used for everyday activities. This keeps them spiritually clean and free from negative vibrations.

Step One: Place a straight-back chair on which you can sit comfortably facing east in the middle of the room. In front of the chair, place a small table with the candle on it. Then, on the floor and around the chair and table, inscribe a thin salt circle.

Step Two: Seat yourself in the chair within the salt circle, light the candle, and use your basic meditation exercise to relax.

Step Three: When you feel completely relaxed, begin to visualize a pure white light descending and encircling your meditation area, making a protective cone from the base of the circle to about three feet above your head. As the cone descends, it will appear as a thin veil of cool mist, much like that which rises off lakes and ponds during the early morning hours. Once the cone is in place, you will feel very light. Your head and shoulders will tingle slightly, and you will experience a profound sense of well-being.

Step Four: When the cone of protective white light is completed and in place, say the following blessing:

> *Blessed Sacred Spirit of all origin, thou art understanding,*
> *compassion, and wisdom. I pray, pour forth your blessing*
> *upon me, that I shall gain insight, wisdom, and knowledge*
> *from your holy presence. Be my protector. Banish all negative*
> *thoughts, vibrations, and visions from thy presence. Let only*
> *your message of higher reflection pour forth, so that I shall*
> *gain enlightenment. So Mote It Be!*

Step Five: Now that you have created the proper atmosphere and are protected, begin to draw your spirit guide to you as follows. Visualize the white light which fills your circle as having a doorway. This doorway is shrouded in a mist. In the mist you see a shadowy figure. As the figure moves toward the doorway, invite it to come to the edge of the circle, but not into the circle.

As the image comes closer it becomes more dense, and you can feel its vibration. Begin to speak in a low, soft tone, one of friendship and welcoming.

Relax, don't be frightened; allow the image to connect with you on a mental level. This is how you will receive messages from your spirit guide. This is the most important and crucial moment of spirit contact. Try to maintain control and don't become startled or jerk around, because sudden movement will disturb reception and cancel out any incoming messages.

Your spirit guide is a loving soul who has chosen to stay behind on the Astral Plane, wishing only to help you in your quest for knowledge. Its obligation is to you, and to help you reach your highest potential. There are very few ways in which your spirit guide can communicate with you, and one of these is through meditation. If you wish to avail yourself of your spirit guide's knowledge, then you must learn to contact it. Once a line of communication has been established between you and your guide, you must learn to listen with your mind.

Allow yourself a few moments of friendly counsel with your spirit guide. This will help establish a good relationship between the two of you and make future communication much easier. When the time is up, you will need to thank your spirit guide and then "ground and center." Ground and center is an exercise in which the participant releases energy back into the earth through a simple focused meditation. It can also be used to draw energy into oneself for a magickal purpose. Use your breath to relax. Visualize a stream of pure energy coming up from the ground into your legs and flowing up and through your body. The energy is usually concentrated in one of the chakras (Chapter 15). To release the energy, use your breath to relax and allow it to flow back, down through your body into the ground.

Step Six: When the session has come to an end, thank your spirit guide with this simple devotion:[3]

---

[3]The devotion or prayer can be one of your own making; just be sure to write it down. It is best to use the same devotion each time, at least in the beginning.

> *Thank you, most compassionate one, who dwells upon the*
> *Astral Plane. I bid thee now, take thy leave and go in peace.*
> *I ask, before you depart, to bless and protect me and guide*
> *my thoughts and actions. So mote it be!*

Step Seven: Ground and center by taking three deep breaths. Now visualize the white light which fills the circle forming a cone above your head. Feel this cone funnel the white light energy down through the top of your head, passing through your spine, out your feet, and back into the ground.

Your meditation is now ended. At this point, you should write down any messages you received in your notebook. It is always a good idea to keep notes on all your magickal activities whether meditation or magick. By doing this, you always have a record of what you did and its outcome for future reference.

Creative Visualization

Creative visualization is the key to success and personal power. It is the name for the process, or technique, Witches use to make their dreams and wishes come true. In essence, creative visualization is a fancy name for the old children's game of "pretend."

What occurs is that the Witch creates an image in his or her imagination of a person, place, or thing which they desire to have or to be. This image is then empowered through meditation and acted on during ritual. The psychic energy directed toward the mental image causes it to physically manifest.

Creative visualization works very well and is easy to do when approached from a realistic point of view. The big mistake most people make with creative visualization is working for things which are not in their realm of availability. By this I mean working for things which are not obtainable rather than for things which are. For example, it would be a waste of time for a clerk in the mail room of a large corporation to use creative visualization to get the CEO's job. This would be out of his range of experience and therefore out of his realm of availability. Even if he were able to get the job, which only happens in the movies, he wouldn't be able to hold it.

I know what you are thinking: Why bother doing magick and creative visualization if you can't use it to get what you want? The answer is simple. Every time you use magick and creative visualization, you expand your realm of availability, putting you that much closer to your goal. Eventually, your magickal successes will bring you within range of getting exactly what you want.

Let's use that mail clerk again (we will call him Joe), as an example of how creative visualization really works. The company Joe works for has hundreds of employees, all of them seeking promotions. The first thing Joe does is to get promoted from mail clerk to mail room manager. This puts him in a position where he can apply for jobs outside his department. By using creative visualization, Joe manages to get an assistant's position in the production department. Once in the production department, more opportunities are available for promotion. With creative visualization, Joe is able to work his way from production into sales, and eventually up the ladder into administration. All of this from his meager beginning in the mail room.

Of course, with time and effort, anyone could accomplish what Joe did. This is true, but the big difference is that Joe did it in half the time. For the average person just plugging along, this type of corporate ladder-climbing would take five to seven years, but by using magick and creative visualization, Joe accomplished this seemingly impossible task in just two years. This is why magick and creative visualization are so important and powerful. They have the capacity to accelerate the creative process.

As with everything in magick, there are some guidelines for making creative visualization work. These guidelines are expressed in the Witch's mystical triangle, and are, in essence, qualities which must be developed in order for creative visualization to be effective.

Belief

Desire   Visualize

Guideline One: Belief

This is a very important guideline. The more you believe in your goal or object of desire, the more likely you are to achieve it. There is a saying, What you believe can happen, you can make happen.

Guideline Two: Desire

You must have a strong desire. This does not mean sitting around and wishing for this and wishing for that. This means you must be totally, passionately, thoroughly engrossed in your desire. It must be so strong that it will take precedence over all other things. You must be obsessed with your goal so as to stir the emotions into action.

Guideline Three: Visualization

For creative visualization to be successful, you must be able to create a clear mental picture of your desire. You must be able to duplicate an exact image of your desire in your mind, just as if you were looking at a photograph of it. This can be very difficult, if not downright impossible, for the average person. This is where good meditation techniques come in. Through discipline and practice, everyone can learn to create visual images in their mind.

Being able to actually see, within your mind, what you really want to have or do is the key. If you really want that job

promotion, you must be able to see it. You must be able to close
your eyes and see your boss calling you into his or her office.
You must see, feel, and hear everything as if it were actually happening. You must be able to create a mental picture so strong that
it will affect its counterpart on the Astral Plane, and through
sheer power of the will, force it to be made manifest.

Thoughts and Ideas

The key to powerful magick lies within your ability to visualize
desires so strongly that the emotions will them to happen. When
the emotions are strong, clear, and focused, then manifestation of
desire is achieved. Wishful thinking alone will not bring about
desired results. You have to really believe that you can truly make
things happen the way you want them to. There can be no doubt,
lack of desire, or impotent emotion involved. Everything you have
must be put into your visualization work to bring it about.

Before you can control the outside forces which dictate your
successes and failures, you must first learn how to control yourself. You must learn how to restrain and keep your emotions in
check. You must possess the ability to focus, with laser-sharp
accuracy, your attention and psychic energy toward the object
of your desire. In any given situation, you must be able to act
with the serene composure of a seasoned professional. You must
develop the attitude of one who knows, without doubt, that
through determination and courage all things are possible.

The meditation exercises presented in this chapter will help you
train your mind and prepare it for doing magick. They are important, because it is through meditation that all things are brought
into perspective. By searching, examining, and analyzing everything
you have been conditioned to believe, you learn in time what is of
value and what is not. This process allows you to clean out the
closet of your mind, and once cleared of all the old garbage, the
mind is then ready to absorb new and better concepts. It is ready
to create a new and better way of life. It is then ready for magick.

3

Symbols of Magick and Mastery

> The whole visible universe is but a storehouse of images
> and signs to which the imagination will give a relative
> place and value; it is a sort of pasture which the imagi-
> nation must digest and transform.
>
> —Charles Baudelaire (1821–67)

Symbols are the fabric from which we form a fundamental
understanding of life and our relationship to the universe. They
are an intrinsic part of the communication system which is
essential to all magickal traditions. Symbols are important because
they convey, in a nonverbal manner, the essence of individual
knowledge and emotion in conjunction with desire.

Magickally, as well as mundanely, symbols are used to create a
bridge, or connection, between the conscious and the subconscious
mind. They reveal and veil certain realities and truths, according to
each individual's level of understanding. Because of their ability to
both unite and separate higher levels of consciousness, symbols have
become the primary language of most Wiccan and mystical systems.

Symbols and images are what link the thought and the creation processes. The emotional response they evoke aids in the focusing and directing of energy. During most magickal operations, symbols are used to represent specific requests as well as mystical concepts. Because of their suggestive capabilities, symbols are the tools Witches use to manifest their desires.

Symbols and tools have a twofold objective: first, they elicit automatic reactions; second, they channel creative energy toward a specific goal. It is this drawing from within and then expressing outward which allows the Witch to recreate reality. No matter what anyone says, symbols, tools, or props are vital to the practice of Witchcraft and magick.

THE FUNDAMENTAL TOOLS OF WITCHCRAFT

The wand, athame, chalice, and pentacle are the four major symbolic tools used by nearly all Wiccan and magickal traditions. They represent individual physical attributes and the elements of nature, and define stations of life. These weapons of psychic wisdom also make a statement about their owner and his or her magickal resolve. In time, with care and use, these tools literally become extensions of the Witch's magickal authority and power.

TABLE OF SYMBOLIC CORRESPONDENCES FOR TOOLS

Wand	Sword	Chalice	Pentacle
air	fire	water	earth
intellect	ambition	emotion	expression
spring	winter	summer	fall
birth	life	death	regeneration
ideas	action	nurturing	manifestation
blue	red	green	yellow
circle	triangle	crescent	square

The Wand

In practice, the wand is the primary working tool of the Witch. It represents his or her rod of power and authority. During ritual, the wand becomes an extension of the Witch's magickal jurisdiction. Personal power is forced through the wand, with laserlike intensity, toward a specified target. When the psychic energy and target meet, activation occurs, and the Witch's intentions are set into motion.

The wand, like every magickal tool, has a distinctive character and represents a specific action, thought, or emotion. In Witchcraft, the wand is associated with the element of air, which is symbolic of the mind, the intellect, and communication. It provides the Witch with a means of channeling abstract thought-forms—as well as energy—onto the material plane. Once the thought-form takes shape and is energized, it will become the medium to manifest desire.

The main reason why the wand is so popular is due to its simplicity. There is nothing complicated or difficult to understand about its construction or purpose. The wand is simply a tool for channeling energy from the spiritual plane to the material plane.

The Athame

The athame is a double-edged knife which is used to inscribe, or cast, the circle of power onto the earth or floor. It is associated with the element of fire and represents strength, power, and the masculine force of nature. Because it is a weapon in every sense of the word, the athame also has the power to subdue or banish rebellious entities or spirits.

Athames, like wands, are used for directing personal power. They help focus energy in a desired direction for a specific purpose. The athame also regulates, as well as conducts, the flow of internal expression toward the desired destination during magickal operations.

The important thing to remember about the athame is that it is a magickal weapon. Like all magickal tools, its value is experienced symbolically on the material plane, but its elemental vibratory rate is expressed on the Astral Plane. This connection between the world of reality and the realm of the spiritual is what gives all symbolic tools their magickal power and potential.

The Chalice

The chalice is feminine in nature and represents the element of water. In ancient times, it was perceived as the cauldron of divine

inspiration, rebirth, and fertility. From a mystical point of view, it symbolizes the womb of the Great Mother Goddess from which all things are born and to which all things return at death.

Most Witches believe that the chalice, like the grail, contains the great mystery of death and regeneration. It embodies the hope and promise of that which is attained when all has been set to rest. It is, at once, open to observation while concealing the mystery which dwells beneath its surface. One needs to delve deep within in order to truly discover what secrets it holds.

The chalice is usually filled with wine and placed on the left side of the altar. At some point during ritual, the athame is plunged into the chalice, blessing its contents. Once the liquid in the chalice has been consecrated, it is consumed by the individual doing the magick, or also by those participating in the ceremony.

The Pentacle

The pentacle is associated with the element of earth and symbolizes the feminine ability to create. On a mundane level, the pentacle embodies the essence of materialism and the ability to escalate secular objectives. It is literally the Witch's canvas on which abstract thought-forms are brought to life. From a spiritual or esoteric viewpoint, the pentacle represents the realm of birth, life, death, and renewal.

In its original form, the pentacle was the shield of the ancient hunter and warrior, and was viewed purely as a defensive weapon. Symbolically, keeping in mind that symbolism is the language of magick, it is not a weapon of war, but one of peace. It is because of its association with the shield that the pentacle became a symbol of protection and a tool used to ward off psychic attack.

During nearly all magickal rites, the pentacle is used as the point of convergence. The desire's symbolic representation is placed on the pentacle, and then all raised energy is focused toward it. The pentacle acts like a magnet, drawing energy toward it, infusing whatever is on top of it with psychic power. Once the symbolic object has been charged or activated, it will begin to work on manifesting the desired outcome.

The Altar

The altar is of extreme importance because it provides the foundation, or form, on which to build and execute magickal operations. The altar is where all obeisance is directed and focused during magick and ritual.

In an esoteric sense, the altar is an extension of your mind and creative process. This is where the substance of thought takes physical form. The altar allows you to express, symbolically, that which you wish to bring about. In other words, it allows you to stand back, look directly at your intentions, and view the whole picture from an objective point of view.

The altar becomes the stage on which you arrange ideas in physical form, using tools and symbols. Each item you place on the altar, including the altar itself, embodies a segment of your extended ability, power, and ambition in symbolic form. The altar displays both your object of desire and anticipated results.

Altars, like people, come in all shapes and sizes, with no two alike. For the outdoor enthusiast, a large flat stone or tree stump may serve as an altar. The picnic basket with a flat top has the ability to store magickal tools and serve as an altar as well. If you are cramped for space, a nicely carved chest or end table with drawers could be the answer. Even folding trays and tables can be used for altars.

The Book of Shadows

The Book of Shadows is not the leather-bound tome of ancient script usually depicted in the movies—you know, the one secreted

away in the back of a musty old book store, the one which is always discovered by the aging eccentric just in time to stop the demon from devouring the virgin. The Book of Shadows is simply a personal journal which contains all of the rituals, spells, and formulas you, as a practicing Witch, gather during your magickal adventures.

The reason for the book's ominous name comes from a time when secrecy was mandatory for survival. People wishing to practice their time-honored traditions in a repressive world had to keep their spiritual beliefs to themselves. So, in privacy, surrounded by the shadows of night, the Witch kept a diary of her magickal enchantments. Because the book contained mystical secrets, penned by the veil of night, it soon became known as the Book of Shadows.

The Book of Shadows is one of the most important tools you have. It will jog your memory during ritual, remind you of past mistakes, and counsel you in times of need. Every ritual, recipe, incantation, magickal spell, or tidbit of wisdom you discover should be recorded in your Book of Shadows.

As with all your tools, simplicity is best. For the most part, leather-bound books of parchment are beautiful, but not very practical. You really need something you can work with, which is why I suggest you get a heavy-duty three-ring binder and section it off with tabbed dividers. Keep plenty of paper in each section so you can take notes when inspiration strikes. Even if you have a computer and keep all your documents on a disk, you are still going to need a printed copy to work from during ritual.

The Censer

The censer can be anything from a simple chafing dish to an elaborate brass incense burner. The censer is sometimes used in conjunction with the wand to represent the element of air. It has long been believed that prayers and wishes are delivered to the gods by way of incense smoke. Because of this, herbal offerings and petitions are often burnt in the censer to aid in love, prosperity, and success spells.

The Element Bowls

The element bowls are two small bowls set on the altar. One of the bowls contains the element of salt and the other the element

of water. The elements are combined and used to bless and consecrate sacred space, symbolic tools, and even participants during ritual.

The Robe

The robe is considered by some Witches to be an optional item. However, I believe it plays an important role in creating the

proper atmosphere for ritual. Just by putting on your robe you automatically switch from the world of mundane activity to the realm of spiritual expression. It is best if the robe is made from dark-colored material, which will not be distracting during ritual. The style and design of the robe should allow for freedom of movement and not present a hazard when working with candles. Long flowing sleeves and elaborate trains are beautiful to look at but get in the way when you are working in small, confined spaces.

The Cauldron

The cauldron is one of the oldest tools of magick known to humankind. It comes to us from the dawn of time and is the birthplace of magickal myth and legend. There was the famed Cauldron of Cerridwen, in which the magic elixir of knowledge and rebirth was concocted. There was the Undry, the cauldron from which everyone was fed according to their station. Finally, there was the famed cauldron of Bran, which gave life to the dead.

The cauldron has many uses, both symbolic and magickal. It can be used to cook and brew herbs, potions, and spells, thus infusing them with symbolic feminine energy. From a practical standpoint, it makes a wonderful receptacle for housing charged objects. The longer they are kept in the cauldron, the more they become charged with the intuitive qualities of the feminine mystique.

The Enchantment of the Spirit Cauldron

The spirit cauldron is an oracle of communication designed to summon forth the wisdom of the spirits on the Astral Plane. It is used for psychic reading as well as for speaking directly with your personal spirit guides. Once the spirit cauldron has been activated, it will serve you well for years to come. Like all of your magical tools, the more you use it, the more powerful it becomes.

To make your spirit cauldron, you will need the following items:

- A medium-sized black cauldron.

- A handful of earth from each of the following places: outside your entry way, the closest cemetery, the closest crossroads, the closest wooded area, and the ocean or a river.

- A small branch from each of the following trees: a tree in your yard, an oak tree, a rowan tree, a willow tree, and a hazel tree.

- A stone dug from deep within the earth, a bird feather, a piece of coal, a seashell, and a small oval-shaped mirror.
- A crystal, a citrine, a bloodstone, an aquamarine, and a hermatite.
- A spoonful of each: mugwort, borage, galangal, yarrow, sandalwood.
- A new deck of Tarot cards or a set of Rune stones for divination.[1]

Step One: On the night of the full moon, fill your cauldron with the required items listed above. Take your time and carefully place the objects in the cauldron as they have been called for. As you do this, think about what they symbolize to you.

Step Two: Place the cauldron in front of your altar. Cover the altar with a white cloth and place the following items on it: one white candle, the censer, smudge and psychic power incense,[2] and salt and water bowls. Begin by blessing your cauldron with the Ritual of Consecration (see page 39).

Step Three: When you are finished with the consecration ritual, take the white candle and place it in the middle of the cauldron (carefully set it on the top of the contents) and say the following:

> *Spirits of the night, see my magic flame*
> *Awaken within the womb from where all came.*
> *As the moon grows full and shines from above*
> *Charge this oracle with truth, power, and love.*
> *So Be It!*

[1]Divination is a "gift from the divine," information received from God. The ability to receive this information is considered a gift, a process or ritual performed with natural things or objects to foresee the future. Tarot cards, Rune stones, bones, dice, a crystal ball, or any number of objects may be used for the purpose of prophecy.

[2]To make psychic power incense, grind together equal amounts of orris root, bay, mugwort, and myrrh, and then add two drops of jasmine oil and one drop of ylang-ylang oil. Keep in a covered container.

Step Four: Light the psychic power incense and blow it into the cauldron until it is filled with smoke. Once the cauldron has filled with smoke from the incense, say the following:

> *Spirits of the air and this dark hour*
> *Fill my cauldron with your psychic power.*
> *Show me the way the future to foresee.*
> *In accordance with your will, so shall it be!*

Step Five: Sprinkle some water and salt into the cauldron as you say the following:

> *Spirits of the sea and earth*
> *To my visions now give birth.*
> *The future I beckon thee me show*
> *That in truth and wisdom I shall grow.*
> *Let now your powers come to me*
> *For this is what I need, so mote it be!*

Step Six: Allow the candle to burn for one hour, then snuff it out and remove it from the cauldron. Put the candle aside and use it when you are doing divination. After each divination session, always return your cards or Runes to the cauldron and thank the spirits in your own words for helping you.

The Stang

The stang is made of wood and is similar in size to that of a walking staff. It is masculine in orientation and corresponds by height to the individual using it. The difference between a staff and a stang in their structure. The staff is usually made from a long straight branch which is tapered or pommeled at the top. The stang is made from a long forked branch, with two prongs at the top, which resemble a pitchfork.

The stang represents the horned god and the masculine force of nature. When the stang is placed with the cauldron, it creates its own altar. It is used for raising or directing power, calling forth the elements, and on special occasions for inscribing the magick circle in the earth.

The stang is one of those tools most people overlook or don't even both with. This is a shame, because the stang can be such a potent and powerful tool when used on a regular basis. It is totally masculine in nature and amazingly impressive when decorated and given a position of power. The stang also adds a quality of the power of majestic sovereignty when used to call in the guardians during ritual.

When the stang is accompanied by the cauldron, it represents the totality of the life-giving properties of the masculine and feminine powers of the universe. Together, the stang and the cauldron create their own altar of power, where energy can be raised and offerings placed in honor of the ancient ones.

Stang Magick

Making a stang is not difficult and definitely not expensive. Plan a trip to your local woods or state park. Be sure to bring along some fresh fruit and flowers to leave as offerings for the woodland spirits.

When you enter the woods, ask the spirits who dwell there to help you find the branch which is right for you. Be sure to tell them exactly what you are looking for and why. Once you have found the perfect branch—and you will find it—be sure to leave the flowers and fruit as a thank you offering. It is always wise to leave a token of appreciation in exchange for the gifts provided by Mother Nature.

Once you have your stang, you should clean it and cut it to size.[3] You will then need to bless and consecrate it, just as you have done with all your other tools. During the consecration ritual, you must shod your stang with iron. This is accomplished by pounding an iron nail into the bottom of the stang. This will prevent its energy from leaching out and back into the ground, as it is believed that psychic power cannot traverse iron.

Your next project is to find a permanent spot for the stang near your altar, where it can be reached easily during ritual. It should always be present when you are working magick, as it will absorb and retain energy. It is good idea to use the stang when calling in guardians or working with the elements, because it is so closely aligned to the natural forces of the land.

The stang is a great tool to use for charging and empowering special objects. I use it to hold a prayer pouch in which I place magickal tokens for power, protection, or success. Because the stang has been shod, the energy it absorbs during ritual will remain within it. However, when something is attached to the stang, it acts like an electrical conduit, passing its energy through to the connected object, charging it with the attributes of masculine strength and power.

The Rituals of Purification and Consecration

All material objects attract psychic vibrations. Sometimes the vibrations are positive and useful, other times they are not. Every competent Witch knows it is unwise to mix psychic vibrations. This is why, before using any symbolic tool for magic, the discerning Witch cleans and purifies his or her tools. Though you can't see the negative energy, that doesn't necessarily mean it isn't present.

---

[3]The stang is usually made to measure the height of the individual using it. So if you are five feet and five inches, then your stang will be five feet and five inches tall.

Even if you make all your own tools from scratch, you still have to get your base materials from someplace. What if the copper tubing you bought to make your wand was previously handled by someone filled with hate and anger? If you do not cleanse and purify the wand once it has been constructed, that negative energy is still within its core. Anything you direct the wand at will be infused with your vibrations as well as those still present in the wand itself.

Self-Purification: The Ritual Bath

Before every ritual or magickal act, you should take a cleansing (ritual) bath. This is important because it will physically, as well as psychically, wash away all negative thoughts and vibrations of the day. The bath also gives you time to relax and think about what you will be doing.

For the ritual bath you will need a white candle, sandalwood incense, and some salt. Into your bath water, pour about 1/4 cup of salt while saying:

> *The power of salt and water now combine to purify and cast out all impurities and uncleanliness of this world. So Mote It Be!*

Now light the candle and incense, and say:

> *As earth and water purify my body, so air and fire cleanse my spirit. So Mote It Be!*

Take your time. Feel the salted water wash away all the negative thoughts and vibrations you picked up during the day. Breathe in the incense and feel it cleanse and purify your thoughts. Look at the candle flame and allow it to lift your spirits and fill you with renewed energy for your magickal works.

When you are finished with your bath, change into your ritual robe. While you are dressing, be aware of how the robe feels next to your skin. Allow the robe to transport you from the mundane world to that of mystery and magick.

Area or Room Purification

Once you have cleansed yourself of the negative thoughts and vibrations of the day, you will want to cleanse the room or area in which you will be performing your magick rites.

Set your altar in the center of the area where you will be working and cover it with a clean white cloth. On the altar, place your censer (with a lit charcoal in it), your two element bowls (one filled with water, the other filled with salt), a white candle, and a container of smudge.[4]

Light the white candle and place the smudge on the charcoal in the censer. Walking widdershins[5] around the area or room, fan the smoke of the smudge as you say the following:

All negative thoughts are banished
All unwanted vibrations are gone.
Only the forces and powers I wish
Will be with me from this moment on!

Return the censer to the altar and pick up the bowl with the salt in it. Sprinkle some of the salt into the water bowl. Stir the salt and water mixture with your finger to mix it thoroughly.

---

[4]Smudge and smudging: smudge is the shaman's term for burning sage; smudging is when you use the smoke from the burning sage to cleanse your aura, magickal tools, and working area of negative vibrations. Sage has cleansing qualities and dissipates negative energy when it comes in contact with it.

[5]Widdershins: counterclockwise. Widdershins movements are used to dispel negative vibrations and energies. Widdershins is also used to cancel out or negate positive movements and actions.

Now, walking deosil[6] around the same area, sprinkle the salt and water mixture, saying:

> *Salt and water now combine*
> *To create my sacred shrine.*
> *None shall enter without my grace*
> *For this now is my sacred space.*

The act of smudging will physically clear the area of all negative energy. You will immediately feel the difference. The air in the room will become fresh and clear. The entire area will feel very clean, as if it were brand new and just being used for the first time.

The Ritual of Consecration

This ritual serves a dual purpose: first, it will remove all previous thoughts and vibrations which might be attached to your tools; second, it will charge each tool with your own personal energy. Once cleaned and charged, the tools will become extensions of your magickal personality. To properly perform this ritual, you will need the following items:

Two white candles
Element bowls filled with salt and water
Smudge or sandalwood incense
Athame, wand, chalice, and pentacle
Altar covered with a white cloth

Begin the consecration as follows:
Light the altar candles (right first, then the left) as you say the following:

---

[6]Deosil: clockwise, believed to be the direction the sun moves. Deosil movements are used to attract or bring in beneficial and positive energy forces. I use deosil to consecrate or build a circle and widdershins to banish or discharge its energy when I am finished.

> *Let now the powers of life and light*
> *Bless and protect me on this night.*

Light some incense or smudge as you say the following:

> *Let now the forces of air and fire*
> *Combine, create, manifest desire.*

In turn, take each one of your tools and sprinkle salt and water over it, saying:

> *O Blessed powers of the earth and sea*
> *Cast out from this tool all negativity.*

Beginning with your athame (followed by each of the tools), hold it high in salute, then consecrate it with each of the four elements. This is accomplished by passing it through the flame of the candle, then the smoke of the incense, and then sprinkling some salt, and then some water on it, saying each time:

> *Forces of Good, of life and of light*
> *Descend into my . . . this night.*
> *For this be a tool of the sacred art*
> *So your powers I ask you now impart.*
> *With the elements of earth, air, fire, and sea*
> *I now baptize, bless, and consecrate thee!*
> *As I Will, So Mote It Be!*

As you bless and consecrate each tool, use your powers of visualization to see and feel the power of the white light, in the form of a bright beam, descending into each tool.

When you have completed passing each of the tools through the elements, take a few moments to reflect. Then, as you snuff out the altar candles, ask this blessing:

O Mighty forces of life and light
Bless and protect me from this night.

Thoughts and Ideas

Magick is a process which promotes transcendental growth and skill. It involves the manipulation of the natural forces of the universe through external direction. When properly worked, magick makes it possible to focus and direct personal energy for the re-creation of reality.

When observed from a pragmatic perspective, magick is the intellectual approach, or method employed by the Witch, to deal with problem situations. The symbolic tools, like the athame and wand, are the implements used to carry out the physical action associated with the reflective process. The ritual is the space in time in which intellect and action come together to help manifest a desire.

The primary tools used in almost every ritual work are the wand, athame, chalice, and pentacle. These symbols of occult jurisdiction are used to charge the thought-forms, which will ultimately produce the magickal reactions mandated by the magician. These tools not only represent occult concepts, they also provide the practitioner with the means to control his or her mental energy. The tools are symbolic as well as physical representations of archetypal concepts; they allow the Witch to bridge the gap between the world of matter and the world of spirit. This ability to move between worlds is the foundation of all magickal power.

Learning to use your symbolic tools effectively is paramount to becoming proficient in the art of Witchcraft and magick. Each time you pick up your athame to cast the circle, or use the wand to charge a talisman, you infuse it with personal power. Even though some of the energy passing through the tools is used for ritual, some of it always remains within the tool itself. Therefore, the more you use your tools, the more energy they will store and the more powerful they will become. After all, personal power[7] is what Witchcraft and magick are all about.

---

[7]Power is the ability to control one's life, and those outside forces which hinder or impede its progress. There is an old expression, "the more power you have, the less you need to use it." If you are a powerful person, and in control, then there is no need to bully others.

4

Air, Fire, Water, and Earth

What canst thou see elsewhere which thou canst not see here? Behold the heaven and the earth and all the elements: for of these are all things created.

—Thomas A. Kempis (1380–1471)

The world we live in is a combination of many forces working together to maintain life. These forces are comprised of both physical (chemical) and metaphysical (spiritual) elements, which are fundamental to the creation process and essential for supporting life as we know it. We need to understand these principle forces if we are to understand ourselves, the universe, and the dynamic energy which controls it.

The principle forces are the four basic elements of Air, Fire, Water, and Earth. These elements are responsible for the structure of this world and other basic phenomena. In general, most Witches and magickal practitioners consider these elements to be symbolic representations of the energy that radiates from the natural world as well as from various archetypal[1] sources.

On the physical plane, we see these elements as air, fire, water, and earth. Symbolically, they represent the intellect, determination or drive, feelings or emotions, and creation and formulation. They give us the ability to reproduce in physical form what we mentally desire. These four elements are facts of life and come to us as fresh air, energy from the sun, water to drink, and the food which is provided by the earth. From a symbolic standpoint, they represent qualities and conditions which we need to observe in order to align ourselves with the natural universe.

It is crucial in the practice of magick to have a thorough knowledge and understanding of these basic elements. Natural magick always seeks the avenue of least resistance, which is represented by the middle path of equilibrium. This middle path enables the mind and body to work in unison, which then provides a direct channel from which creative energies can flow. Once the individual begins to work with the elemental energies, he or she once again becomes attuned to the delicate rhythms of nature. Then, and only then, is he or she able to manipulate the subtle forces of the universe.

Learning about the elements and the areas of life they control is an important part of all magickal training and development. Once you begin to harmonize with these magickal forces of nature, you become aware of their knowledge and wisdom. The insight you gain from interacting with the elements will bring your material and spiritual worlds into alignment. Once you have control over your thoughts and actions, you will be able to harness your Witch power and direct your energy toward the manifestation of desire.

Take some time to look around and see how the elements are associated with almost everything. They correspond to the seasons

---

[1]Archetypal: a basic form or pattern on which all objects of a certain category are built. Prototype: an ideal example of a type.

of the year, the days of the week, plants, heavenly bodies, and even precious stones and metals. Without a doubt, the elements are among nature's greatest contributions to the magickal world of Witchcraft. They are a wondrous storehouse of knowledge just waiting to be tapped.

Working With the Elements

No matter who you are or where you live, in one way or another the elements affect your life. Air, Fire, Water, and Earth are everywhere, there is just no way to avoid their influence. However, there are ways to work with these forces of nature so they balance out within the mind and body. Balance, or mental equilibrium, is a goal most Witches strive to reach.

To really get to know the elements, it is necessary to feel them, work with them, and use them in daily life. By incorporating these four natural elements into your daily routine, you actually begin to "live" magick rather than just observe it. This is important, as Witchcraft (or any philosophy) is useless if it cannot be applied to life and bring about desired results.

The best way to learn about the elements is to work with each one individually. Begin by working with the element of Air. Spend an entire week focusing on the magickal quality of Air. Buy a bell, hang wind chimes, make a wand, or just spend time looking at the sky. When you have finished working with the air element, move on to the element of Fire, then Water, and finally Earth.

The Element of Air

Air provides us with inspiration, illumination, and the ability to communicate our ideas to others. It allows us to access the realms of the spirit and domains of deity. Through music, poetry, and narration, we are able to explain, as well as express, our true nature.

Like all of the elements, Air is nonjudgmental. It has both a negative as well as positive side. Words spoken in haste, curses voiced in anger, and vicious gossip are the negative sides of Air. Spiritual musings, poetic enchantments, and humanitarian efforts are the positive sides of Air.

In the practice of magick, the element of air relates to the East, the home of inspiration and knowledge. It occupies the etheric world between the physical and spiritual plane. The Air world is inhabited by mystical creatures called sylphs.

The sylphs are often depicted as diminutive fairies with diaphanous wings and bodies. They are responsible for all the movements of Air, from the slightest breeze to the mightiest hurricane. The sylphs are summoned when problems with communication and creativity arise. However, it should be remembered that sylphs are, above all, elemental powers, which can be as vicious when abused as they can be beneficial.

Air Correspondences

Value:	Inspiration, illumination, awareness, perception
Color:	Blue, silver, white, and gray
Symbols:	Circle, bird, bell, sylph, flute, chimes, clouds
Tools:	Wand, Rod, Staff
Plants:	Almond, broom, clover, eyebright, lavender, pine
Stones:	Amethyst, sapphire, citrine, azurite
Places:	Sky, mountaintops, treetops, bluffs, airplanes
Zodiac:	Aquarius, Gemini, Libra
Time:	Spring, dawn
Archangel:	Raphael
Direction:	East
Process:	Thinking, reading, speaking, praying, singing

Experience is always the best teacher. The following exercise will provide you with the experience necessary to integrate the elements into daily life. It is the use of these subtle forces of the elements which will help you align your consciousness to that of the cosmic order. This in turn develops your self-control, giving you power over your mundane nature.

For this exercise and those that follow, you will need to choose a symbol to represent each element. This can be something for which you already have an affinity,[2] or you may pick one from the list following the descriptions of each element. Either way, the symbol with which you will be working should be one which represents the true nature of the element. The idea here is to have a physical representation of the concept with which you are working, something you can hold or look at. This is important, because later on you will be learning how to transfer energy from yourself into physical objects, creating personal links for magickal works.

Exercise One: Working With Air

Sit quietly and relax as you do in your general meditation exercise. Hold the Air object in your hand; look at it. Use your breath to control your thoughts. Breathe in to a count of five and then exhale to a count of five. Do this several times until your concentration is fixed upon the object. Feel the object become light, so light it could float. Because you are holding it, you, too, are so light you can float.

Feel yourself floating upward toward the blue sky, so lightly that you drift like a feather in the wind. Feel the sun and fresh air upon your face as you float higher and higher. As you soar above the ground, feel yourself as totally free and able to do anything you wish.

While you are in this place look around: What do you see? How do you feel? What thoughts present themselves? Keep floating, feeling free and able to do as you wish. It is during this time

---

[2]An affinity is a feeling toward something special to you, maybe a favorite Tarot card, a crystal, a smooth stone, a shell you picked up from the beach, any object which will put you in touch with the element.

that original ideas will come to you. Remember those ideas; they represent your higher consciousness and its creative ability. These thoughts are what you should be working on. These are the things the real you wants to do, create, and complete. Take them with you as you begin to descend.

Slowly float downward until your feet touch the earth and you begin to feel the weight of your body. You are now in total touch with reality and have the knowledge of your Air journey to help guide you toward your desired goal.

The Element of Fire

The untamed forces of nature have always been a source of great mystery and fascination. Of all the elements, Fire is one of the most commanding. It is at once the ultimate Creator and Destroyer. Fire can provide light and warmth, or cause devastating disaster. Fire may be quick to respond and slow to extinguish, but it is always compelling. Fire is pure raw power which holds little compassion for anything other than itself.

Fire will forever be regarded with enduring reverence because it has the ability to summon respect from all who cross its path. The powers which are manifested in its blazing passion are analogous to the vital life forces which pulse through the veins of the universe.

Fire, like all aspects of nature, has a negative as well as a positive side. Its positive countenance expresses faith, courage, and enterprise, the negative side is anger, fear, and violence. Fire's ultimate purpose is transformation through expurgation.

In the practice of magick, the element of fire relates to the South, the realm of energy and power. The awesome potential of Fire is realized in the flames of a blazing bonfire, the lustful passions of embrace, or through the disciplines of strenuous endeavor.

The torches which illuminate the mystical regions of Fire are watched over by the invincible, golden-eyed salamanders. The salamanders are the fire-starters of nature. They appear as small dragonlike creatures with blazing tongues, piercing eyes, and razor-sharp claws. The salamanders are responsible for all fire, from the smallest spark to the most devastating volcanic eruption. They are in charge of maintaining the temperature of the earth and should be respected for their awesome powers.

The salamanders, like the physical element they represent, should be approached with caution. Fire is raw primitive power, and as such behaves according to its nature. From a volcanic explosion to the most ravaging and unmerciful forest fire, Fire remains unbridled power.

The element of fire promotes transformation and purification. Fire is the life-giving generative powers of the sun. From Fire we receive intensity, aspiration, and personal power. It is the force which motivates and drives all living organisms. It represents personal willpower and the force which sparks creation.

Fire Correspondences

Value:	Energy, transformation, strength, power, courage
Color:	Red, red-orange as in flames, amber
Symbols:	Triangle, lightning, flame, the salamander
Tools:	Sword, dagger, firepot, double-headed axe
Plants:	Basil, bloodroot, dragon's blood, ginger, orange, tobacco
Stones:	Ruby, garnet, diamond, bloodstone, flint, sunstone
Places:	Volcanoes, ovens, fireplaces, deserts
Zodiac:	Aries, Leo, Sagittarius
Archangel:	Michael
Time:	Summer, noon
Direction:	South
Process:	Passion, anger, impetuousness, progression, valor

Exercise Two: Working With Fire

Sit quietly and relax as you breathe in and out to the count of five, and control your thoughts as you did in the previous exercise. Holding or looking at the Fire symbol, feel yourself growing hot; feel the heat and energy of the fire element flow through your body. Feel yourself being totally engulfed in flames, yet not being harmed in any way. You are all-powerful; you have the energy and ability to accomplish anything you wish. You are strong, forceful, and filled with energy.

Point your fingers and see the flames shoot from the tips. See these flames turn into energy and power, power that allows you to move things without touching them. See the pure energy of life being projected from the tips of your fingers.

Now, taking the ideas that were given to you during your Air journey, see yourself doing these things. Make things happen through your own personal power and energy. You are as the flame—hot and powerful, and you can do what you set out to do. You burn with passion and power and the will to accomplish your goals. Allow this impression to be burned into your consciousness.

Slowly feel the warmth begin to cool. Slowly come back to reality while still retaining that sense of personal power, the knowledge of your ability to manifest your desires.

The Element of Water

Water has long been seen as the source of all potentials in existence. It is associated with the Great Mother, the universal womb, birth, and fertility. Water is emblematic of the life-giving and life-destroying abilities of the cosmos. Water is vital to our survival and without it we would perish. From the smallest drop of rain to the depths of the ocean, water responds to our needs. Water brings nourishment to the land and refreshment to people.

Water is emotion, intuition, and the ability to heal. It expresses its nature through love, transition, and personal awareness. Being neither vaporous nor solid, water is located midway between heaven and the earth. It is fluid and encourages the qualities of moderation. Water cools the anger brought on by too much fire, and it stabilizes the illusions caused by an excess of Air.

The refreshing and cleansing powers of Water are seen in the early morning dew, felt in the first showers of spring, and assimilated during the practice of ritual bathing. The water element is closely guarded by the ever powerful, and yet remarkably elusive, undines.

Half aquatic and half human, the undines rule over two-thirds of the earth's surface. They reside within all bodies of water and resemble a fish with a human torso.

The undines are associated with the emotions and sensuality. They are ever willing to help their human counterparts develop emotional stability and sensitivity. When angered, their passions rise, as do the waters they control. Flooding and drought are the punishments leveled against humanity for its deliberate disregard of Mother Nature's passionate undines.

Water Correspondences

Value:	Emotion, intuition, devotion, the mystical
Color:	Green, turquoise
Symbols:	Crescent, shell, boat, ship wheel, anchor, cup
Tools:	Vessel, grail, chalice, cauldron
Plants:	Aloe, cucumber, dulse, gardenia, lily, lotus, willow
Stones:	Aquamarine, chrysocolla, moonstone, mother-of-pearl
Places:	Oceans, rivers, lakes, ponds, waterfalls, beaches
Zodiac:	Cancer, Scorpio, Pisces
Archangel:	Gabriel
Time:	Autumn, sunset
Direction:	West
Process:	Love, nurture, sensitivity, psychic ability, healing

Exercise Three: Working With Water

Relax and use your breath to control your thoughts. Holding or looking at your Water symbol, begin to feel cool, clear, fresh water surrounding you. You are floating on top of the waves. It is restful, quiet, and you can see the clear blue sky overhead.

Slowly allow the water to cover you; begin to sink beneath the surface of the water until you are completely immersed in it. Do not be afraid. Like a fish, you are completely at home. Swim around under the surface of the water. See the other fish, plants, and underwater growth. Feel how calm and quiet everything is. You are totally aware of everything around you, yet nothing can harm you or disturb your sense of peace. The water is absorbing your problems, your negative thoughts, and giving you a feeling of deep emotional security.

You know that no matter what happens to you, water will be there to help restore your vitality. It will provide you with the rest you need to help regenerate and reorganize your thoughts. This is a time of total quiet, when you can really reach deep inside and feel your whole being, a time to learn how your emotions react, a time to get in touch with the real you. When in the water, you are safe from the outside world, so you can take time to just *be*.

Slowly float to the surface. See the sky above as you begin to get out of the water, feel the warmth of the sun and the cool breeze as it refreshes you. Be sure to remember how you felt while you were in the water. Take this feeling of being totally, psychically, and emotionally clean and refreshed with you. Know that when you begin to get emotional about something you can wash this feeling away with the water element.

The Element of Earth

Where would Air, Fire, and Water be without Earth? Earth is the foundation on which Mother Nature has built Her wondrous world. Earth holds, nourishes, and affirms. Earth sees, touches, smells, senses, and feels. Earth is both sensual and practical. Earth can be stubborn as well as generous. Earth has instinct, rather than feelings, for the cycles and seasons of time.

It is slow, steady, and ever changing, while remaining true to its own nature.

Earth is Mother Nature's great repository. Earth contains everything humans need to survive, prosper, and grow. Earth provides us with a place where we can partake of the essence of spirit, relish in the wonders of life, and delight in the passions of love. Earth is our home and we should respect it.

The earth symbolically represents both the womb and the grave. Earth is the element that brings forth life and then reclaims it. Magickally, Earth is viewed as the final outcome, a place where the other elements can physically manifest their nature.

Guarding the earth and all her wonders are the precocious, yet ever watchful gnomes. The gnomes are the oldest of Mother Nature's creations. Bent and gnarled like the ancient oak, these spirited dwarflike creatures protect the land and all that lie upon it. The gnomes live in the forest among the roots of giant trees, and deep within the hollow hills.

The gnomes' job is to protect the physical structure of the earth. Gnomes are traditionally associated with healing because they have knowledge of all plants and their medicinal properties. In times of failing health, the gnomes are summoned for their expert assistance. When annoyed with humans, the gnomes strike back through earthquakes, landslides, and pestilence.

Earth Correspondences

Value:	Responsibility, perseverance, experience, authority
Color:	Yellow, brown, russet
Symbols:	Square, cornucopia, spindle, scythe, salt
Tools:	Shield, pentacle, flail, horn
Plants:	Alfalfa, cotton, oats, patchouly, vetiver, wheat
Stones:	Moss agate, jasper, malachite, peridot, tourmaline
Places:	Caves, forests, fields, gardens, canyons

Zodiac:	Capricorn, Taurus, Virgo
Archangel:	Auriel
Time:	Midnight, winter
Direction:	North
Process:	Responsible, practical, organized, steady, grounded

Exercise Four: Working With Earth

As before, relax and use your breath to control your thoughts. Hold and look at your Earth symbol. Visualize a cave set deep within the earth. Now enter the cave, allowing your eyes to adjust to the dark. Then proceed to go deeper and deeper into the cave, downward, spiraling downward, ever deeper.

Hear the trickle of an underwater stream which travels through the cave. Look at the cave walls. What do you see? How do you feel? What impressions about yourself do you get in connection with being in the cave?

Look up and see a tiny slit, far above. See the shaft of light coming through to light the way, revealing the cave's inner depths. Look and see the crystals and different-shaped rocks, the pale green moss that carpets the floor. Everything has beauty and elegance, the kind of beauty that only Mother Nature creates.

Breathe deeply, feel the heavy earth-scented air enter your body, giving you strength and vitality that you haven't had before. Feel the cave floor beneath you. Pick up a handful of the dark moist earth; look at it, feel it, smell it, absorb its richness. Feel your connection to the earth and know you are a part of it. Allow the life-giving qualities of the earth to penetrate you, giving you strength and reassurance in your abilities.

Be still, reflect on the cave and the total protection it provides. Now slowly begin your journey back. Before leaving, say a little prayer to the Earth Mother. Thank her for this time of solitude and take the security of earth energy with you.

Thoughts and Ideas

No matter who you are or where you live, the elements in one way or another affect your life. The elements are everywhere, and there is no way to avoid their influence. However, there are ways to work with them so they balance within the mind and body. Reaching balance and a point of mental and physical equilibrium is necessary if you are going to be effective as a witch or in life in general.

Every time you work with the elements, you reawaken your connection to the natural world, where everything is possible. When you invoke the potential of Air, you awaken your imagination and inspire new thoughts. When you conjure the power of Fire, you gain inner strength and awareness. As you learn to control the forces of Water, you begin to gain control over your emotions. Once you are on good terms with Earth, you will discover that you have the ability to manifest your desires.

Working with the elements can be fun, as well as educational. Choose one day a week to work with each element. A good example would be working with Air on Wednesday. Wednesday is ruled by the planet Mercury, which is directly associated with communication. You might try wearing something yellow that day, and make an extra effort to speak out about your ideas. Or, you could try working with the element of water on Monday. Monday is associated with the moon, the Goddess, and the water element. Wear green clothing and silver jewelry. Try using the Water meditation exercise to get in touch with your emotions and clear away internal conflicts. By working with the elements on a regular basis, you integrate magick into your daily routine, and it automatically becomes part of your life. (For more information about color magick, see Chapter 11.)

5

Circles of Light

The circle exists on the boundaries of ordinary space and
time; it is "between the worlds" of the seen and the
unseen, of flashlight and starlight consciousness, a space
in which alternate realities meet, in which the past and
future are open to us.

—Starhawk, *The Spiral Dance*

Witches, Pagans, and practitioners of the magickal arts have always
used the circle as their place of spiritual reflection. By virtue of
its nature, the circle has become a universal symbol of totality,
wholeness, and original perfection. It has no beginning and no
end. It is, in itself, the unmanifest, the infinite eternal and a time-
enclosed space. It represents celestial unity, cyclic movement, and
completion. The circle is feminine and serves to contain, as does
the womb, all life and energy raised within it. It also provides a
limit, or boundary, in the creation of sacred space.

Once the circle has been properly consecrated, it serves a twofold purpose. First, it acts as a boundary to keep out negative

forces and retain positive ones. Second, the circle serves as a meeting place for spiritual and magickal activities. The circle is the perfect pattern for regulating people who are attempting to work together or exchange energy.

To the Witch, the circle is a sacred space where magickal operations can be performed safely. Before all rituals, the Witch will physically mark out the circle on the floor. He or she will then ritually empower the circle to be a protective barrier between "the world of men and the realm of the Mighty Ones." Safe within its boundary, the Witch is free to conjure and create his or her own alternate reality.

Working With the Circles

Creating sacred space is an essential part of all magickal operations. The physical act itself takes the form of casting or constructing a magick circle. This is done in order to create the proper environment for magickal works and rites. Once the magick circle has been created, it will protect the individual within its boundary from outside negative influence. The circle, or boundary, will also help contain the energy raised within its periphery until the time of release.

The first thing you will want to do is to clearly mark out a circle on the floor. The ideal size of a magickal circle is nine[1] feet in diameter, but while this is ideal, it is not mandatory. In most cases, the size of the circle will depend on available space and the amount of people taking part in the ritual. Obviously, five to seven people will fit nicely into a nine-foot circle, but fifty will not.

The actual marking of the circle can be done in a variety of ways. If the floor is carpeted, you can mark the circle with tape

---

[1]Nine is composed of the all powerful 3×3; it is the triple triad and represents completion, fulfillment, attainment, beginning and end, the whole—some of the same symbolism of the circle itself.

or string. Hardwood, cement, or tile can be marked with light-colored chalk. If you are working outside, you can circumscribe the earth with your wand or athame. For those fortunate enough to have a special room set aside for their magickal practice, the circle may be painted directly onto the floor itself. A large piece of indoor-outdoor carpet cut into a circle serves nicely and can be rolled up when you are finished. Seasonal representations, such as flowers, pine cones, or small sprigs of greenery can also be used to designate the circle's periphery. The important thing is not so much what you use, but the setting of a physical boundary line.

Once the circle is marked, you will also want to acknowledge the four quadrants, or elemental directions, with a symbolic representation. The four quadrants represent the four elements of nature and their respective energies. The East is Air, intellect, and new beginnings; the South is Fire, power, and the force within; the West is Water, emotion, and rebirth; the North is Earth and the ability to manifest desire. The following list will give you some ideas of objects which can be used:

- East: an incense burner and a joss stick or cone incense, a blue candle, a large piece of amethyst, the star card of the Tarot, a blue circle.

- South: a candleholder with a red candle, a garnet or blood-stone, the strength card of the Tarot, a red triangle.

- West: a goblet filled with water, a green candle, aquamarine or green tourmaline, the death card of the Tarot, a green crescent moon.

- North: a square wooden box with a pentacle engraved on the top, clear quartz crystal, a yellow candle, the hierophant card of the Tarot, a yellow square.

Place the objects symbolizing the quadrants on the floor outside of the circle in the appropriate direction. Use small tables or

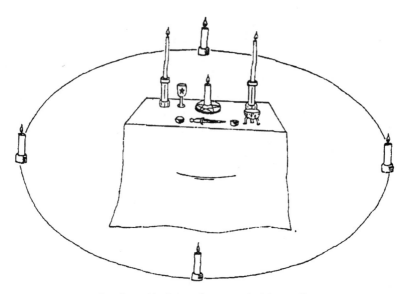

An altar with the quadrants marked by candles

boxes to hold the items, or place them on wall shelves which correspond to the proper direction.

Once you have the circle and directions physically set, place the altar inside of the circle. The position of the altar within the circle is up to the individual, however, most practitioners tend to favor keeping it in the center, facing either the north or east. North represents the realm of the gods and manifestation; the East is new beginnings and the realm of the spirit. By placing the altar in the center of the circle, it automatically becomes the focal point of the ceremony, where all energy and power is directed. As the altar represents the core of your desire, its central location will only enhance the work at hand.

The next step is the actual casting of the magick circle. This is accomplished in two steps: first is the consecration of the elements (salt and water); second is the projection of energy onto the marked circle. These combined actions produce the proper atmosphere for a ritual. It is important to understand that as you project the energy onto the physical circle you are in reality creating a sphere or total enclosure, rather than just a flat line of energy. When a circle is properly cast, it resembles a large crystal globe of luminous light.

Casting the Circle

Take your athame or wand and dip the tip into the water, saying:

> *Creature of Water, cast out from thyself all impurities and uncleanliness of this world.*

Dip your athame or wand into the salt, saying:

> *Creature of Earth, let only good enter to aid me in my work.*

Stir three scoops of salt into the water, and see with your mind's eye all the negative energies leaving. Now, holding your athame or wand in front of you, begin to visualize the energy, in the form of a blue flame, coming through into the point of the wand or athame. Begin walking in a deosil (clockwise) manner, pointing your athame or wand down at the edge of the circle as you say:

> *I conjure and create thee, O circle of power. Be thou a boundary between the world of men and the realm of the Mighty Ones. Be thou a sphere of protection to preserve and contain all powers raised within. Let now this circle be a place of peace, love, and power. So Mote It Be!*

With the casting of the circle completed, you will then want to acknowledge the four directions, or quadrants. This can be done in several ways. Whether the method be simple or complex, the idea is to enlist these specific energies to guard and protect your circle. There will be two methods described. The first is a simple acknowledgment of the quadrants and is done prior to the casting of the circle. This method can be used for personal works, or those in which the circle itself serves as the majority of protection.

Acknowledging the Quadrants

For this particular method, you will need to have candles at each of the quadrants: for the East, blue; the South, red; the West, green; the North, yellow.

Stand before the altar and take several deep, relaxing breaths. When you feel composed and ready, proceed to the Eastern quadrant with a lighted taper. Pick up the Eastern candle, and light it as you say the following:

> *I light the East, the home of moonlight and consciousness,*
> *the realm of the spirit.*

Now proceed to the South, and light the candle as you say the following:

> *I light the South, the home of fire and inspiration, the realm*
> *of awareness,*

Now proceed to the West, and light the candle as you say the following:

> *I light the West, the home of the waves of completeness, the*
> *realm of our watery beginnings.*

Now proceed to the North, and light the candle as you say the following:

> *I light the North, the home of all that is green and fruitful,*
> *the realm of remembrance.*

Now return to the altar, consecrate the elements, and cast the circle.

Calling the Guardians

The following procedure is for the actual calling in of protective Guardians. Guardians are highly evolved soul minds attached or attracted to the earth's vibration. They can be seen as archangels (etheric world intelligences who have always existed) or higher-energy forces in alignment with archetypal elemental forms. This ritual to call in the Guardians is usually done for full moon rituals and sabbats, or any time a great amount of protection and extra energy is needed.

For this, you will need four candles, one for each quadrant in its corresponding color, and something symbolic[2] to represent the quadrant as well. Once the circle has been cast, return to the altar. Take several deep breaths, relax, and then proceed to the Eastern quadrant (again walking deosil) with your athame. Point the athame upwards in the direction of the quadrant and visualize the Guardian approaching.

Light the blue candle and say:

> *Hear me, O Mighty One, Ruler of the Whirlwinds,*
> *Guardian of the Eastern Portal. Let your essence be as one*
> *with me, as witness and shield at this gateway between the*
> *worlds. So Mote It Be!*

Hold the Eastern symbol in offering, replace it, and then proceed to the South. Light the red candle of the South and say:

> *Hear Me, O Mighty One, Ruler of the Solar Orb,*
> *Guardian of the Southern Portal. Let your light be as one*

[2]Symbolic objects: East, wand, incense, or bell; South, sword, candle, or sun symbol; West, chalice, cauldron, or shell; North, rock, crystal, or pentacle.

with me, as witness and shield at this gateway between the
worlds. So Mote It Be!

Hold the Southern symbol in offering, replace it, and then proceed to the West. Light the green candle of the West and say:

Hear Me, O Mighty One, Ruler of the Mysterious Depths,
Guardian of the Western Portal. Let your fluid be as one
with me, as witness and shield at this gateway between the
worlds. So Mote It Be!

Hold the Western symbol in offering, replace it, and then proceed to the North. Light the yellow candle of the North and say:

Hear Me, O Mighty One, Ruler of the Forest and Field,
Guardian of the Northern Portal. Let your fruitfulness be as
one with me, as witness and shield at this gateway between
the worlds. So Mote It Be!

Now hold the Northern symbol in offering, replace it, and return to the altar. Hold your athame directly above your head and forcibly announce the following as you visualize your protective sphere glowing and radiating with power.

I command the powers of Light and Dark. For as Above, so
Below. As the Universe, so the Soul. As without, so within.
Let now this rite begin. So Mote It Be!

At this point, your magick temple is erected and sacred space has been created. Once inside your circle, you will not want to step outside it until your ritual is completed, the Guardians dismissed, and the circle has been dissolved. As with all magick, there is a reason for staying within the bounds of your consecrated space. The most important reason is that a properly erected circle forms an energy barrier between you and the outside world. When the barrier is crossed, it will break. Once this happens, the wall of protection you created has a hole in it and the energy raised within escapes, or even worse, the negative, outside energy comes in. In either case, this can create an unfavorable atmosphere.

Dismissing the Guardians and Banishing the Circle

What goes up must come down, and so it is with the circle of power. It takes as much time and energy to disassemble the circle as it does to erect it. This is something to bear in mind when you are working within a specific time frame. Always be sure to proportion your time wisely and leave plenty for dismissing and taking up the circle.

The following method is for dismissing the Guardians and taking up the circle. This is done to release and clear the area of raised vibrations and energy.

You will begin in the North and proceed widdershins (counterclockwise) around the circle. This is a very effective way of taking things down. It allows you to retrace your steps and make sure that everything has been brought to a proper closure.

Take several deep breaths, relax, and then proceed to the Northern quadrant (walking widdershins) with your athame. Point the athame upward in the direction of the quadrant and visualize the Guardian returning and leaving as you say:

> *Hear Me, O Mighty One, Ruler of Forest and Field,*
> *Guardian of the Northern Portal. I thank Thee for thy*
> *blessings and protection and bid Thee hail and farewell.*

Now put the Northern candle out and proceed to the West.

> *Hear Me, O Mighty One, Ruler of the Mysterious Depths,*
> *Guardian of the Western Portal. I thank Thee for thy*
> *blessings and protection and bid Thee hail and farewell.*

Now put the Western candle out and proceed to the South.

Hear Me, O Mighty One, Ruler of the Solar Orb,
Guardian of the Southern Portal. I thank Thee for thy
blessings and protection and bid Thee hail and farewell.

Now put out the Southern candle and proceed to the East.

Hear Me, O Mighty One, Ruler of the Whirlwinds,
Guardian of the Eastern Portal. I thank Thee for thy
blessings and protection and bid Thee hail and farewell.

Now put out the Eastern candle and proceed back to the altar. You will now want to take up the circle. Begin in the North and proceed in a widdershins direction around the circle, this time drawing the energy back up into your wand or athame:

O circle of power that has been a boundary between the
world of men and the realm of the Mighty Ones, that has
served to preserve and protect, I now release all powers raised
within and banish thee, O circle of power. So Mote It Be!

With the eradication of the circle, the rite is brought to a close. If you do not have a special room set aside for ritual, it is a good idea to get into the habit of putting your magickal tools away immediately. Another suggestion is a postritual celebration. Many Witches like to have a feast, or meal, following ritual. This helps to ground the energy raised during the ceremony, and is especially helpful in getting to sleep if you have worked late into the evening.

Thoughts and Ideas

There are as many ways to create a magick circle as there are Witches to cast them. It is recommended to test several methods before making a final decision as to which way is best. I prefer to cast the circle the old-fashioned way, using the method previously described. However, this does not necessarily mean that this method is the only way to do it. There are many Witches who prefer using the sword instead of the athame or wand. This is a customary practice, especially among ceremonial magicians. Then there are those who prefer to focus on the elements of Earth and Water rather than on a specific tool when casting. This is a perfectly acceptable way to consecrate sacred space. The important thing to remember about casting a circle is how you focus your attention, not how you handle a magickal weapon.

Some Witches do not even use the wand or athame to cast the circle. Instead, they will take a branch of hyssop or angelica, tie it with colored ribbon, and dip it into the salt and water. When the branch is sufficiently wet, they will sprinkle the mixture around the circle as they say:

> *All negative thoughts are banished*
> *All unwanted vibrations are gone.*
> *Only the forces and powers I wish*
> *Shall be with me from this moment on.*

This same idea, or method of casting the circle, can be done by using smudge and a mixture of salt and water. To use the smudge method, begin by walking around the circle with a bowl or stick of smudge. As you walk around the area of the circle, say the following:

> *All negative thoughts are banished*
> *All unwanted vibrations are gone*
> *Only the forces and powers I wish*
> *Shall be with me from this moment on.*

Next, mix the salt and water, which should already be on your altar. Proceed around the circle, sprinkling the mixture on the ground. As you walk around the circle, say the following:

Salt and water now combine
To create this sacred shrine.
None shall enter without my grace
For this now is my sacred space.

When the above is completed using either method, you have ritually sealed off sacred space. Your circle is cast and ready for your magickal rites to begin. When you are finished, reverse the method and use the branch of hyssop, angelica, or Witch's broom to banish the energy of the circle. Simply walk widdershins around the circle, sweeping away the energy as you say:

I banish thee, circle of power
Protector of my rites this hour.
Energy raised now shall disperse
And return to the Mother Earth.
So Shall It Be!

Simple, yet effective, these methods for casting the circle work very well. The reason these methods work is because they are forthright in their wording and easily done. You do not need complicated rituals or "eighty-dollar words" or thousand-dollar athames to be a Witch. All you really need to make Witchcraft and magick work is a sincere belief in your craft, a strong will, and an adventurous spirit.

Part II

The Practice of
Modern Witchcraft

6

Beneath a Silver Moon

There is something haunting in the light of the moon;
it has all the dispassionateness of a disembodied soul, and
something of its inconceivable mystery.

—Joseph Conrad (1857–1924), English novelist

There have been vast amounts of research done on the moon, detailing its effect on both humans and the environment. It has been credited with the curious power of being able to change humans into beasts, vampires into bats, and the most cautious people into passionate lovers. Because of the moon's awesome powers, it has long been a familiar accomplice of the consummate Witch.

The moon, like the sun, rises in the east and sets in the west. Unlike the sun, the appearance of its size and shape continually change, at least from our earth-bound perspective. In a lunar month there are four cycles of approximately seven days. The phases the moon goes through include the Dark of the Moon (also called the new moon). It waxes and grows larger until the first quarter is visible as the half moon. Then the moon continues to wax, or

Dark (New)   First Quarter   Full   Last Quarter

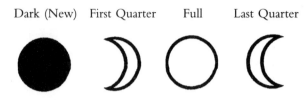

grow larger, and its horns point to the east until it reaches a full circle, known as the full moon. It will then begin to diminish in size as it wanes through the last quarter, with the horns pointing west, and continues to wane until the new moon returns.

Most Witches will tell you that knowing the phases of the moon is an important part of their craft. Rituals always work best when they are in agreement with corresponding lunar and planetary energies. It is important to time magickal operations according to the phases of the moon so that you stay in sympathy with the natural pull of the universe. By doing this, you combine natural outside energy and power with your own energy and power. When doing magick, the more circumstances you can bring into harmony with what you are doing, the better the results will be.

By looking at the phases of the moon one at a time, we see an inherent working pattern evolve. The period from the new moon through the first quarter is usually referred to as the waxing moon. This is the best time to begin new projects and work toward obtaining something on a positive level.

During the full moon, projects already begun are energized, nurtured, and reaffirmed. This is also a time when most Witches meet to worship the Goddess in her mother aspect.

The period from the last quarter to the dark moon is a time of contemplation, reflection, and negation. This time is associated with the release of negative energies. It is a good time to consider our actions, rest, and regenerate the mind and body. This phase of the moon is aligned to the west and the north. The period of the dark moon is a very good time get rid of things which are negative, a time to let go of petty judgments and hatreds, cleanse, and purify our surroundings.

There are many ways to work these combinations. I like to begin with the dark moon, which is the time just before the new moon. This is a good time to get rid of negative energies which may surround me or my goal. Then, when the new moon arrives, I am able to begin working on something positive, without the influence of unwanted vibrations. I will then use the full moon to emphasize and reaffirm that which I have already set in motion. Finally, the last quarter is used for contemplation and gives the goal time to manifest.

A good example of this can be seen when people wish to bring love into their life. During the dark moon they should work on getting rid of their personal fears about love. Or, if they were doing a ritual to attract someone they already knew, they should use this time for dissipating their fears about love and relationships. When the moon begins to wax, they should work on becoming more attractive to the other person, or building self-esteem. On the night of the full moon, they should put all of their energy into proclaiming their desire and determining how the loved one should see or react to them.

Each full moon has a specific designation and symbolic meaning. As can be seen by the following list, these meanings are obviously connected to the hunting and agricultural seasons of our ancestors. However, just because their meanings appear slightly antiquated does not necessarily make them obsolete. Energy is energy, and though we may not be using it for the procreation of the tribe or a bumper crop of corn, we can surely use it for the advancement of intellectual and spiritual endeavors.

The Full Moons

November (Snow Moon): Scorpio brings in the dark season and winter begins. This is the death of the season and time to get rid of negative thoughts and vibrations.

December (Oak Moon): The mighty oak withstands the cold hardship of winter. The oak is revered because of its longevity and the fact that such a mighty creature comes from the smallest acorn. Now is the time to remain steadfast in convictions and principles.

January (Wolf Moon): The wolf is a fearsome creature of the night as well as a companion to the Witch and Shaman. The wolf protects and guards his home and family. This is a time to protect what we have as well as consider new options.

February (Storm Moon): A storm is said to rage most fiercely just before it ends and the year usually follows suit. The end of winter, and death and darkness, is coming. It now is time to plan for the future and what we will pursue in the months to come.

March (Chaste Moon): All is fresh and virginal as life begins anew. This marks the end of winter and uncertainty. Now we can begin to plant the seeds of desire.

April (Seed Moon): Spring is in the air; all is green and speaks of growth. This is the time of sowing seeds (spiritual or corporeal) and the time to physically put our desires into motion.

May (Hare Moon): The hare is a sacred symbol of springtime and fertility. With all life blossoming about us, the creative spirit now takes over as we reaffirm our goals.

June (Dyad Moon): Dyad is the Latin name for pair, the twin stars of Castor and Pollux. This is a time of equality, the union of opposites, and duality, the time to seek balance between our spiritual and physical desires.

July (Mead Moon): Mead was the traditional beverage of our European ancestors. This was a time for working to preserve some of those crops (mostly for wine- and ale-making) for winter and future use. It is the time to plan for what we will do when we reach our goals.

August (Wort Moon): Wort is the Anglo-Saxon term for "herb," or "green plant." This is the first harvest, and a time to celebrate as well as work toward reaching our goal. Plans for preserving what we have attained should be considered.

September (Barley Moon): We enter the sign of Virgo, the virgin who carries sheaves of barley and grain. This is the Great Harvest, a time for celebration and realization of desired goals.

October (Blood Moon): This moon marks the season of hunting and the slaughter of animals for winter food and clothing. Blood is the force of life. Now is the time to offer up the reddest of wine in thanksgiving for what we have attained.

The Planets

The phases of the moon are not the only things to keep in mind when planning the best time to do magickal works. The seven days of the week and their corresponding planetary affiliations are also of great importance. The list presented here outlines the natural magickal correspondences of these astrological energies.

Sunday (Sun): This is a day of high masculine solar energy, a very powerful time, and one good for individual, positive, creative works. Begin things related to acquiring money, health, friendship, and patronage for business. The element for Sunday is Fire; the color is yellow gold or gold. The numerical consideration is one or six. Marigolds, sunflowers, and goldenrod are associated with this planetary influence, as well as the precious metal gold, the diamond, topaz, and tiger's-eye.

Monday (Moon): This is a day of high feminine energy. A very powerful time for matters concerning conception, the development of emotional self-expression, seeking inspiration, enhancing psychic abilities, initiating changes, and personal growth of the feminine aspect. The element for Monday is Water; the color is silver or white. The numerical consideration is nine. Watercress, jasmine, and moonflower are associated with this planet, along with the metal silver, the moonstone, pearl, and clear quartz crystal.

Tuesday (Mars): Dynamic energy is the only way to express Mars. Pure raw power and intense activity. This is a good time to overcome rivalry or malice, develop physical strength and courage, or protect one's property and investments. It is a good time for military matters or anything which requires a lot of force, power, and energy to activate. Very masculine in gender and warlike in presentation. The element for Tuesday is fire; the color is red, vivid blood red. The numerical consideration is five. Wormwood, pepper, and garlic are associated with this planet, along with iron, the bloodstone, ruby, and garnet.

Wednesday (Mercury): Communication is the key for Mercury. This planet wants to be heard and will aid you in getting your ideas out there; good for business deals and helping to influence others—very career oriented. The element for Wednesday is air; the color is yellow. The numerical consideration is eight. Cinnamon, horehound, and honesty are associated with this planet, along with quicksilver (mercury), opal, agate, and aventurine.

Thursday (Jupiter): Deals with expansion, idealism, and ambition. Jupiter will help you attain friendship. It is good to use for career success and all situations concerned with money. Legal transactions are best dealt with during Jupiter. Religious expansion is also expressed through this planet. The element for Thursday is water and the color is deep blue or purple. The numerical consideration is four. Cedar, betony, and mistletoe are associated with this planet, along with tin, amethyst, lepidolite, and lapis lazuli.

Friday (Venus): Love and attraction are the key words for Venus. All works involving sensual and sexual attraction are in her domain. It is a good time to create a union between opposites and build good relationships. The element for Friday can be either earth or water and the color is green. The numerical consideration is seven. Rose, basil, and yarrow are associated with this planet, along with copper, rose quartz, emerald, and chrysocolla.

Saturday (Saturn): Formation and the first law of Karma (limitation) belong to Saturn. Here we find the tester, and the principle of learning through trial and error; Saturn should be used to preserve, stabilize, and crystallize our ability to discipline ourselves. The element for Saturday is earth and the color is black. The numerical consideration is three. Hemlock, skullcap, spikenard, and belladonna are all associated with this planet, along with onyx, black tourmaline, obsidian, and jet.

This may look confusing at first, but it is really very simple. The moon tells you when psychic energy is at its peak, and the planets tell you which days are best for specific magickal works. For example, the Friday closest to the full moon would be an ideal time for doing a love spell. The first Wednesday after the new moon might be used for getting a job promotion, while Saturday, during the waning moon, would be an ideal time for eliminating negativity. There is just no end to the possibilities when magick is combined with lunar and planetary power.

Working With the Moon

Just like water, electricity, or any other form of energy, magick travels the path of least resistance. This is why you look for the way which offers the least amount of opposition to your magickal operation. By working with the path of least resistance, you are using your energy effectively and to its fullest potential. The easiest and most efficient way to use magick is through the natural flow of the universe. One way this can be accomplished is through personal alignment with the different vibrational sequences of the moon. When you combine personal power with the power emanating from the moon, you create a potent energy circuit. This circuit is what helps you construct effective thought-forms, which in turn will manifest your desires.

The moon is more than just the sun's reflected glory, it is the majestic personification of the past, present, and future. Even our ancestors noted how the moon's waxing and waning corresponded to the sea tides and the behavior patterns of people, animals, and plants. To the modern Witch, the moon is the mistress of all magick, a symbol of the goddess who rules the night sky, the earth, and all in the land of spirits beneath it.

In Witchcraft, the full moon is a time of immense—and intense—psychic power. When there is a difficult task at hand, there is no better time than the full moon to resolve it. This is why most Witches plan their magickal activities to coincide with the rising of the full moon. They want to take advantage of the moon's power and channel it into their personal magickal works.

When planning a full moon ritual, the first priority is to find out when the moon will be full. The Old Farmer's Almanac or any good astrological calendar will provide you with this information. Once the date and time have been set, you will need to find a place to perform the ritual. If weather and locale permit, then it is best to perform your rite out of doors, directly in the path of the moon's rays. However, if this is not possible, and for most of us it is not, then a quiet corner of a bedroom, or any room, will suffice.

One hour prior to the full moon ritual, physically mark out a circle three to nine feet in diameter with tape or chalk. If you are working outdoors, inscribe the circle into the ground with your wand or athame. Place your altar in the center of the circle, cover it with a white cloth, and set it as usual. Be sure to cleanse the area if you have not used it before. Take time to review the ritual you will be performing, and double-check to make sure you have every thing you need.

The following full moon ritual was designed for the solitary practitioner and focuses on the blessing of magickal tools. It is a good idea to copy the ritual into your Book of Shadows, or onto a separate sheet of paper. This will provide you with printed copy to read, or work from, during ritual. Be sure to add your own personal thoughts, symbols, and petitions where indicated. The more personalized the ritual, the more power it will have. After all, it is your feelings and desires which should be amplified at this time, not mine or someone else's.

Full Moon Ritual

I. Requirements

Time: Full moon of _____ (date and time)

Objective: _____ (what you are working for)

Altar arrangement for a full moon ritual

Standard items required: athame, chalice, carafe of white wine,[1] pentacle, wand, censer, bowls of salt and water, white altar cloth, two white candles, gardenia incense, the Book of Shadows.

Additional items required: _____ (extra items you may want to add to the ritual)

Full Moon Ritual Liturgy

1. Consecrate the elements, cast the circle, and call in the Guardians[2].

2. Light the two white altar candles, starting with the right one, as you say the following:

---

[1]For those who cannot use wine, substitute white grape juice or bottled spring water.

[2]Calling in the Guardians is optional for a simple solitary full moon rite. However, if you feel it is necessary to call in the Guardians, then by all means, do. There is no hard-and-fast rule about this.

Right candle:

> *Lunar Mistress meek and mild*
> > *Look upon your seeking child.*
> *With this candle I now light*
> > *Please bring me joy on this night.*

Left Candle:

> *I now approach Thee of gentle grace*
> > *To bless and protect this sacred space.*
> *With this torch of truth and praise*
> > *Guide me through my nights and days.*
> *So Mote It Be!*

3. Pick up the censer, add incense if necessary, and proceed to the East. Hold the incense in offering as you say:

> *I offer the element of air, for insight and wisdom.*

Return the censer to the altar and pick up the right candle. Proceed to the South. Hold the candle in offering as you say:

> *I offer the element of fire, for strength and power.*

Return the athame to the altar and pick up the water bowl. Proceed to the West. Hold the bowl in offering as you say:

> *I offer the element of water, for control and dominion.*

Return the bowl to the altar and pick up the salt bowl. Proceed to the North. Hold the bowl in offering as you say:

> *I offer the element of earth, for the manifestation of desire.*

Return the bowl to the altar.

4. Facing the altar, with proper reverence, recite the following:

Mistress of Magick, Lady of the Night,
Mother of Mist, Moor, and Moonlight,
Great indeed is your awesome power,
Which illuminates my world this hour.
I ask you keep my heart happy and free,
And bless me with love, health, and prosperity.
For this I will, so let it be!

5. Still facing the altar, bless your tools as follows: Begin with the wand by passing it through the incense smoke and candle flame. Then sprinkle it with salt and water. Now point the wand at the moon, and see and feel the power of the moon flowing into the wand. Bless the wand with the following affirmation:

By four elements born to the night
The Lady's spirit round and bright.
A hidden splendor in the moon-led sea
All that is brilliance and meant to be.
From depths of soul unknown let swell
The moon-born might to power this spell.
Bathed in her glory I now proclaim
This tool is blessed in my lady's[3] name.

Repeat the above procedure with the athame, chalice, and pentacle. When you have completed the blessing, spend a few moments in quiet reflection, meditation, or petitioning favors of your own.

---

[3]If you have a special goddess you work with, you may use her name here.

6. Now pour the wine into the chalice and bless it as follows: Drink the wine in celebration and honor of the Moon Goddess, and say:

> *Elemental Spirits, Lady of the Moon*
> > *Of Thee I ask this simple boon.*
> *Bless this wine and bless this rite,*
> > *Guide and guard me from this night.*
> *So Mote It Be!*

7. Extinguish the altar candles, starting with the left one, as follows:

Left candle:

> *Let now the power, potential, and force*
> > *Return unto the original source.*

Right candle:

> *Let now the motion, direction, and sight*
> > *Return unto the original light.*

8. Dismiss the guardians, if you called them in at the beginning of the ritual, and banish the circle. The rite is ended.

Thoughts and Ideas

A full moon ritual does not necessarily have to be elaborate or complicated to achieve its purpose. In fact, this is where so many make their greatest mistake. They attempt to enlist the power of every conceivable magickal item and incantation known to man. They end up with something resembling an auction at a flea market rather than a practice of the magickal arts. On the other hand, a ritual without the appropriate components, energy, and enthusiasm is just as useless.

Balance is the key to an effective ritual. It means knowing what, when, and where to use your magickal tools and symbols so they are most effective. You don't see a carpenter carrying every tool he owns to the top of the ladder just to nail in a single board. He surveys the job and takes up only what he needs. Witchcraft and magick are no different. You should take time to plan exactly what you want to accomplish and find the appropriate items you need for the ritual. Simplicity, focused attention, and personal reflection are what will make your rituals powerful and worthwhile.

Once you feel comfortable with lunar energy, try working with each phase of the moon separately. During the period from new to full moon, experiment with different types of divination. On the night of the full moon, work magick and cast spells. When the moon begins to wane, observe its affect on meditation and dream-working.

Mix and match your experiments over a three-month period, and then analyze the results. By doing this, you will find which phase of the moon works best for you, when doing divination, magick or meditation. Everyone is different, and what works for me may not necessarily work for you. The only way to find out what works best for you is to experiment with everything.

7

Celestial Forces and Powers

All good fortune is a gift of the gods, and . . . you don't win the favor of the ancient gods by being good, but by being bold.

—Anita Brookner (b. 1938) British novelist, art historian

Since the beginning of time, humankind has looked to the heavens for inspiration. The sun became a god, the moon became a goddess, and their children, the stars, filled the skies. Majestic mountains, winding rivers, underground caverns, and towering trees became their dwelling places upon the earth. Their powers are awesome, their conquests are legend, and their love for mankind is unquestionable. They have not died, they have not gone away, they are only waiting for you to bid them welcome—today.

While this book is not about religion, it does accept the presence of higher forces, those of a god and goddess, within the framework of certain rituals. It is important for the aspiring Witch and magician to learn to connect with these forces, or gods, because of their power and potential. In essence, their sovereignty can be very comforting and beneficial in times of stress or need.

Energy and Deity

Within the universe there are certain levels of conscious energy which have always existed. Our ancestors recognized these special forces and bestowed them with individual identity and human characteristics. By doing this, they were able to relate to them on more of an intimate and personal level. It was this relationship, with these constructs of conscious energy,[1] that eventually produced the various pantheons of gods and goddesses which now exist.

Initially, it is necessary to understand the nature of these energy forces (or gods), and their potential within the realm of Witchcraft and magick. For the most part, the relationship between an individual and a deity is very much like the relationship between the individual and his or her bank account. However, instead of dealing with a bank and money, you are dealing with a god, or energy force.

Think about it: if you want a bank account, you need to choose a bank in which to put your money. Then you open the account by identifying yourself and depositing money into it. At regular intervals, you will put more money into the account. For your consideration of support, and the use of your money, the bank pays you interest. The more money you put into the bank account, the more interest you receive and the more money you end up with. It is the same thing with a god and goddess. You find the pantheon of gods you want to work with, then invest your energy, rather than your money, into it.

[1]Constructs of conscious energy are in essence the original archetypal sources from which humanity constructed its vision, or version, of anthropomorphic divine beings.

Working With Deity

The first step in choosing a god or goddess to work with is to become familiar with their mythological history. This is best done by reading about the gods and goddesses and learning what types of energy they represent. The next step is to select a deity from the pantheon which best represents, to you, the archetypal forces of the universe. The following descriptions of gods and goddesses come from various cultures of the world, and represent a cross section of spiritual ideals to consider.

The Goddess

After centuries of exile, the Goddess has made her way back to her land, people, and position as the personification of feminine dominion and perception.

She is the Earth Mother and Mistress of Magick; she is all that is beauty and bounty. What the God inaugurates, the Goddess materializes. He impregnates her with the seed of desire and she gives birth to reality. The Goddess is the creative process through which all physical levels are manifested.

The Goddess is the intuitive and instinctive side of nature. Her inconceivable powers of transition and transformation radiate like the translucent beams of celestial light, for she is mystery and magick. Beneath her full round moon she has been, and still is, invoked by those seeking her favors as Arianrhod, Diana, Hecate, and by many other names. Everything psychic and mysterious belongs to her alone.

Goddesses From Around the World

Hecate *(Greek and Roman)*: Hecate is one of the oldest embodiments of the Triple Moon Goddess worshiped today. She holds power over the heavens, the earth, and the underworld, where she is in control of birth, life, and death. Hecate is the giver of visions, magick, and regeneration. She can grant the ability of second sight and teach those seeking the deepest secrets of magick. Hecate and her lover Hermes are the guardians at the gates of the underworld, easing the transition from this life to the next. Because of her guardianship at the gateway between the worlds, Hecate is also associated with the crossroads, the meeting place of time and space.

Summon Hecate for psychic power, protection and self-defense, and to banish negative energy.

Correspondences

Archetype	Queen of the Underworld
Expression	Death Crone
Time	Full moon and waning moon
Season	Winter
Objects	Moon, crossroads, triangle, bow and arrow, key, cross, sword or dagger, rope
Number	Three
Colors	Black, dark blue, silver, white
Animals	Hound, bear, lion, snake, horse
Trees	Cypress, poplar, yew
Plants	Mugwort, myrrh, civet, jasmine, lily, patchouly, belladonna, hemlock, mint
Stones	Onyx, star sapphire, moonstone, pearl, opal

Diana *(Roman)*: Diana is a virgin goddess and very protective of her own chastity. She will take revenge on any mortal who crosses her path, or that of her companions in this regard. Diana's

most important feature is her ability to create, which makes her the queen of all sorcery. Under Christian rule, Diana became the goddess of the Witches and Pagans. In ancient times, it was believed that the Witches rode with Diana at night to their secret meetings along with a pack of hounds. Because of this, her cults were condemned around the tenth century, and any found worshiping Diana were, of course, put to death as Witches.

Summon Diana for all works of magick, Witchcraft, or Sorcery.

Correspondences

Archetype	Virgin, protectress
Expression	Mistress of Magick
Time	Full moon
Season	Spring and summer
Objects	Bow, arrow, sandals
Number	Three
Colors	Silver, pearl white, azure
Animals	Bear, hound, dear
Trees	Willow, hazel
Plants	Mandrake, almond, mugwort, moonwort, jasmine
Stones	Quartz crystal, moonstone, pearl, sapphire

Cerridwen *(Celtic)*: Cerridwen is the Celtic mother goddess of the moon and grain. She is especially known for her fearsome death totem, a white corpse-eating sow. Cerridwen is associated with Astarte or Demeter, and her harvest celebrations express her ability to both give life and take it away. Because of her inexhaustable cauldron[2] in which she brewed a magick draught called "greal," Cerridwen is also known as the goddess of inspiration and knowledge. This draught would give inspiration and knowledge to any who drank it.

Summon Cerridwen for spiritual inspiration, magickal knowledge and wisdom, and personal power.

Correspondences

Archetype	Crone, initiator
Expression	Mother of Inspiration
Time	Waning moon
Season	Harvest (winter)
Objects	Cauldron, cup
Number	Three (and combinations of three)
Colors	Green, blue green, silver, or white
Animals	Sow, hen, greyhound, otter, hawk
Trees	Elder, yew
Plants	Corn, barley, hellebore, patchouly, ivy, morning glory, mimosa, belladonna
Stones	Moonstone, beryl, chalcedony

Freya *(Norse)*: Freya, which means "Lady," is one of the most revered of the Teutonic goddesses. She is known as the Fair One, and famed for her great beauty. She is primarily the goddess of love, but does oversee war, life, and death as well. She is a patroness to housewives, mothers, and women of great strength and power. She is one of the demigoddesses who selects the most noble of the fallen warriors, which she will then carry to the realm of the gods. Freya has been known to appear to her worshipers in a falcon-plumed cloak, under which she wears a

---

[2]This cauldron was called Amen. The cauldron is considered to be the symbol of life and death, and regeneration. It is symbolic of the womb and its creation process.

magickal necklace called Brisingamen. The necklace's power cannot be resisted by man or god.

Summon Freya for matters of love, and when personal strength and power are needed.

Correspondences

Archetype	Virgin, lover
Expression	Priestess of Love, Life, and Death
Time	Waxing moon
Seasons	Spring and summer
Objects	Brisingamen, feather cloak, wings
Number	Five
Colors	Silver, pink, pale blue, pale green
Animals	Cat, hawk, boar
Trees	Apple, holly
Plants	Cowslip, crocus, rose, lilac, primrose, sweet pea
Stones	Blue or pink tourmaline, emerald, chrysocolla

Isis *(Egyptian)*: Isis (Greek for Aset), whose name means the throne, is the personification of the Great Goddess in her aspect of maternal devotion. She is the daughter of Seb and Nut, wife and sister of Osiris, and mother to Horus. Myth and legend confirm Isis as the true wife and mother. When Isis's husband Osiris was killed by his jealous brother Set, she spared no pains in finding his hidden body. She then made love with Osiris, conceived, and gave birth to Horus. Isis is worshiped as "the great magick" because she protected her son Horus from predators and other dangers. It was, and still is, believed that because of this, Isis will protect mortal children from the perils of daily life as well.

Summon Isis in matters of love, marriage, for the protection of children, and for help with magickal rites.

Correspondences

Archetype	Mother, protectress
Expression	Mistress of Magick
Time	Waxing moon
Seasons	Spring or summer
Objects	Thet (knot or buckle), scepter, cup, horns, mirror
Numbers	Two or eight
Colors	Sky blue, green, gold, white
Animals	Snake, goose, owl, hawk, ram
Trees	Fig, willow
Plants	Lotus, lily, narcissus, myrtle, myrrh, iris, date
Stones	Lapis, aquamarine, sapphire

Erzulie *(Haitian)*: Erzulie is the goddess of the independent, fulfilled woman. She is the mistress of love, marriage, beauty, abundance, music, and art. All acts of romantic love and pleasure are her delights. Erzulie is the divinity of dreams, the goddess of love, and the muse of beauty. She is the mother of myth and gives meaning to what life holds in secret. She is all that is seductive. Because she can be both vengeful and loving to those who grace her presence, she is also considered to be very mysterious.

Summon Erzulie to dominate another for sexual pleasure or romantic love, to gain great riches, or for lucid dreaming.

Correspondences

Archetype	Virgin mistress
Expression	Eloquence
Time	Waxing moon
Season	Summer

Objects	Fan, rattle, mirror, comb, peacock feathers, three gold wedding bands
Number	Five
Colors	Yellow, coral, pink, red
Animals	Peacock, vulture, parrot
Plants	Pumpkin, orange, cinnamon, allspice, nutmeg, basil, yellow or pink roses, lily, honeysuckle
Stones	Rose quartz, diamond, topaz

The God

Like all deities, the God has many faces. He appears as the radiant, brilliant, and illuminating Sun of Righteousness; the divine victim who spills his blood for the love of the land; the warrior king

whose fight for truth and justice are revealed in the battle between good and evil. To all those who practice Witchcraft, the God is the symbol of virility, the fertilizing and regenerating energy force of nature. He is the personification of all that is masculine, potent, and powerful.

The God's most obvious and dominant characteristic is in his ability to regenerate. Although his countenance may change with time and culture, he continually returns to live and die for the land he loves. He has been known as Osiris, Tammuz, and Adonis. He has become manifest as the Unconquered Sun or compassionate savior Mithra and Helios. Whatever his incarnation, he is always the potentate of power, strength, and authority—and the final judge before the gate of the Goddess.

Gods From Around the World

Hermes *(Greek)*: Hermes is the god of communication, commerce, twilight, and the wind. His Greek name suggests movement, so Hermes is viewed as a guardian of travelers. Images of Hermes are placed where country roads branch and at the crossroads in towns. It is also believed that he escorts the souls of the dead to the underworld along with his lover Hecate. It is because of Hermes' expressiveness and eloquence that Zeus named him god of the spoken word. Hermes is honored by this highly valued position because it is through speech that exchanges are made, gallantries expressed, and knowledge conveyed.

Summon Hermes for problems with communication, when extra knowledge of a subject is needed, and for help with speech.

Correspondences

Archetype	Divine messenger, or trickster
Expression	Benefactor of Mankind
Time	Waxing moon
Seasons	Spring and summer
Objects	Caduceus, flute, lyre, crossroads, staff, wings, feathers, cup, sandals
Number	Four
Colors	Yellow, orange, silver
Animals	Cow, goat, bird, tortoise, lamb
Trees	Olive, palm, mayapple

Plants	Orange, clover, lavender, lily of the valley, lemon verbena, pecan
Stones	Topaz, citrine, quicksilver (mercury)

Zeus *(Greek)*: Zeus was the supreme deity in Greek mythology. He was the son of Kronos and Rhea, and was considered to be the "wise council." As a composite figure, this sky god of the Greeks was active in the daily concerns of the world. Because of his involvement with humankind's affairs, he was venerated as a ruling father figure rather than as a creator deity. Zeus governed the sky and all atmospheric phenomena. He had dominion over the winds, clouds, rain, and the destructive thunder and lightning. He was depicted as a robust and mature man, with wavy or curly hair which matched his thick beard. Zeus often wore a crown of oak leaves, carried a thunderbolt, and had an eagle at his feet.

Summon Zeus for legal matters, court battles, where justice is needed, for resolving political matters, as well as for gaining wealth.

Correspondences

Archetype	Father, ruler, or king
Expression	Ruler of the Sky, King of the Gods
Time	Noon to midnight
Seasons	Summer, fall, and winter
Objects	Thunderbolt, scepter, crown, dagger
Number	One
Colors	Royal purple, dark blue, gold
Animals	Eagle, goat, cuckoo, elephant
Trees	Olive, oak, poplar, alder
Plants	Olive, ambergris, violets, apple, mistletoe, mastic, fenugreek, mint
Stones	Diamond, amethyst, chalcedony

Cernunnos *(Celtic)*: Cernunnos, Celtic god of vegetation, fertility, and the underworld. Cernunnos is the stag god, lord of the beasts, and master of woodland animals. His name means "Horned One" and he is usually depicted with rams' horns and serpents. His horns are symbols of strength, power, and virility. The snakes are phallic and symbolic of regeneration. Cernunnos can be seen as part man and part beast. He is the one who guards the portals of the underworld and ushers those seeking transformation into the mysteries. Like most horned gods, he is concerned with the earth and how human life parallels its rhythms and cycles. Of prime importance is the idea of growing and becoming strong in order to ensure the survival of life and the land.

Summon Cernunnos in matters of survival, when physical strength is needed, during times of transition, and for male virility.

Correspondences

Archetype	Guardian, regenerator
Expression	Father of life
Season	Summer
Time	Full moon
Objects	Torc necklace, horns, cornucopia, stang
Number	Six
Colors	Red, orange, yellow, sometimes black or brown
Animals	Stag, ram, serpent, dog, eagle
Tree	Oak
Plants	Benzoin, bay, mistletoe, orange, juniper, sunflower, marigold
Stones	Agate, jasper, carnelian

Odin *(Norse)*: Odin was sometimes called Woden or Wotan, which probably meant "wild" or "furious." He was the prime deity of the Norse pantheon and respected for his vast wisdom. He was considered to be both a father and victorious warrior. Because of his authority, he was consulted by all of the other gods, as well as human beings. Odin was wise in the ways of the world and possessed immense powers. The myths of Odin describe him as always being involved with the people, taking an interest in their daily lives and helping out in family matters. The thing that seems to set Odin apart from other gods is his quest for knowledge. He treasured it so highly that he gave his right eye for it. He is the ultimate priest for God, and an example to all men because of his ability to gain knowledge.

Summon Odin for help with learning, passing tests, when personal authority is needed, and for winning battles.

Correspondences

Archetype	Warrior, father
Expression	Priest, Shaman
Time	New moon
Season	Winter
Objects	Sword, shield, runes, robe
Number	One
Colors	Gold, red
Animals	Wolf, raven, horse
Trees	Birch, oak
Plants	Holly, mistletoe, juniper, gum arabic, marigold, angelica, mastic
Stones	Diamond, bloodstone, garnet

Osiris *(Egyptian)*: Osiris symbolizes the divine in mortal form. He is the personification of physical creation and its cycles of birth, life, death, and return. He is the highest of all powers, the king who brought civilization to the land of Egypt. He is husband and brother to Isis, father of Horus, and son of Seb and Nut. Osiris was treacherously murdered by his brother Set, who was considered to be the power of evil and darkness. After his death and resurrection, Osiris became the lord of the underworld and judge of the dead. He presides in the seat of judgment, when the heart of the deceased is weighed against the feather of Ma-at.

Summon Osiris in criminal matters, for receiving a fair verdict in court, or for help with creative endeavors.

Correspondences

Archetype	King, priest
Expression	Father of stability and growth
Time	Waning moon
Seasons	Fall and winter
Objects	*Djed*, crook, flail, *menat*, was (scepter)
Numbers	Seven, fourteen, and twenty-eight
Colors	Gold, yellow, green, and white
Animals	Hawk, jackal, ape, bull
Trees	Cypress, thorn
Plants	Acacia, ivy, papyrus, orris, lily, storax, bay, frankincense, dittany
Stones	Topaz, quartz crystal, carnelian

Damballah Wedo *(Haitian)*: Damballah Wedo is the personification of the Da, the universal current of psychic power. He is the dynamic of pure action, of which his own movement is a graphic representation. He is the great father, benevolent, paternal, and compassionate; his followers come to him for blessings as well as for protection. Damballah is the positive force which encircles the universe; he has no malevolent sense. Damballah is at the top of the spiritual hierarchy and is the oldest and most respected of the Haitian gods. Damballah is pictured as a snake arched in the path of the sun. Sometimes half the arch is composed of his female counterpart Ayida Wedo, the rainbow. Together, Damballah and Ayida represent the ultimate totality of sexual unison. They encompass the cosmos and are pictured as intertwined serpents coiled around the world egg.

Summon Damballah to increase psychic power, sexual endurance, and wealth.

Correspondences

Archetype	Cosmic force
Expression	Power of Regeneration
Time	Full moon
Seasons	Spring and summer
Objects	*Asson*, staff, wand, cosmic egg, calabash, sun
Number	Four
Colors	Red and white
Animals	Snake, rooster, ram
Trees	Palm, apple, cola
Plants	Apples, bananas, eggs, cornmeal, cola nuts, yams, coconut
Stones	Ruby, garnet, diamond, quartz crystal

Thoughts and Ideas

The process of connecting with a deity is a very personal one. There is no right or wrong way to do it. It is really up to each individual to decide whether or not he or she wishes to work with a god or goddess. Personally, I feel it is best to use one's own personal power for magick and spell-crafting, and reserve seasonal celebrations for communion with the Higher Forces. By separating practice methods, the difference between celestial sovereignty and personal power is easier to determine.

In selecting a god or goddess, you can approach the process in various ways. Take a good look at your ancestral heritage, as this will provide insight into your cultural conditioning. Use your personal interests or previous religious training to help you decide. Some people find it helpful to study ancient myths and legends, as these seem to inspire and encourage the searching soul.

The most important thing to remember when choosing a god or goddess is to *choose the one you feel comfortable with.* Just because your closest friend is working with Isis doesn't necessarily mean you should work with her as well. If you feel more of an affinity toward Hecate, then this is who you should choose. But no matter who you choose, the choice is yours, and should be based on your spiritual awareness and personal feelings of kinship with the deity. Only you know how you feel and what will best serve your needs.

When reading through the list of gods and goddesses, you will notice that each has been assigned specific, symbolic, correspondences. These correspondences serve as communication links between you and your chosen god form. When you incorporate one or more of these symbolic correspondences into a magickal rite, you are in essence extending an invitation to that deity to join with you. By combining your energy with that of the gods, you intensify the ritual experience and magnify your personal power.

The following suggestions will help you learn to work with the god and goddess of your choice.

- Buy or make a statue of the deity and place it on your altar. Once a day, go before the statue and speak to it, just as you would to a close friend.

- When you are meditating, burn candles in the corresponding colors to the deity statue.

- Make a robe of the primary color which corresponds to your deity. Wear this during your meditations and rituals.

- Make a necklace out of the suggested stones to wear during your ceremonies.

- Use the corresponding plants in the incenses and oils you prepare for use during ritual.

- Place the deity's sacred objects on your altar during ritual.

- Incorporate their symbolic animals into your ceremonies or place pictures of them near your ritual area.

- Combine all of the above suggestions and make a shrine to your deity so the energy is available when you wish to work with it.

When looking to the gods and goddesses, it is important to understand their historical development, even though this may seem irrelevant in today's world. These extraordinary beings were created for a reason and therefore have a purpose. Their myths and legends can help us all to understand the phenomena of celestial movement and seasonal change, and provide guidance in the transitions from life to death. Whatever the situation, there is a god or goddess in charge who can be petitioned for help and advice. The security of knowing there is a superior being in charge of things makes life a lot less frightening.

8

Festivals of Light and Life

> Live in each season as it passes; breath the air, drink the drink, taste the fruit, and resign yourself to the influence of each. Let them be your only diet drink and botanical medicines.
>
> —Henry David Thoreau (1817–62) U.S. philosopher

Witchcraft is a very instinctive way to approach life. Since the craft has such an affinity for the natural world, it places great importance on the concepts of balance and harmony. This becomes quite obvious when we look at how Witches appreciate, and acknowledge, the changing of the seasons.

The modern Witch's calendar, often referred to as the wheel of the year, is divided into eight sections. Each section, similar to the spokes of a wheel, represents a seasonal change. These seasonal changes are called sabbats, and occur approximately every six weeks. The wheel begins with Yule, or the Winter Solstice, on December 21, and ends with Samhain, or Hallowmas, on October 31.

To most Witches, these sabbats are not just a change of season and weather, but are a reflection of the life cycle processes of birth, life, and death. Physically, as well as spiritually, the sabbats represent times of great power and potential.

There are several ways of looking at the sabbats in connection with Witchcraft and magick. One is through the classical myth regarding the lord of life and death uniting with the lady of birth and renewal. Another is through the ballad, in which songs like "John Barleycorn" explain the cycle of life through a series of poetic verses. Probably the simplest way to view these times of power is from the agricultural standpoint.

Using agriculture as our example, we can view the seasons in terms of *planning, planting, harvesting,* and *resting.* In the early spring, the farmer will *plan* his or her crop and garden, preparing to *plant* by late spring or early summer. In the late summer or early fall, the farmer will *harvest* his or her crops. Then, in the late fall through the winter, all is allowed to *rest* and regenerate.

Though most of us are not farmers, and the closest we get to an actual crop is in the grocery store, we can still appreciate the farmer's simple and natural approach toward the work at hand. For example, you would never see a farmer out in his field in August planting a new crop. Even if he or she were able to get the seeds to germinate, in six weeks the frost would kill the small, delicate plants. Witchcraft is the same. If, as practicing Witches, we plan and plant the seeds of our desires at the appropriate times, then our wishes will surely be made manifest. On the other hand, if we attempt to work in opposition to the natural flow, then the rewards of our labors will be slim or nonexistent.

The first thing to do is break the seasons down into eight segments. This will show you the sequence of vibration through which your actions will fall into harmony with those of the universe. Once you begin to work with this natural flow of energy, or vibrational frequency, your magick becomes almost effortless. It will seem as though time has sped up, and what was just a dream a month ago is now a reality.

A good example of going with the flow is walking up the escalator which is moving in an upward direction. You will certainly get to the top faster, and with less effort, than if you just stood still or used the stairs. By combining the power of the escalator with that of your own walking, you reach your destination sooner. However, if you try to walk down the up escalator, you will be going against the flow, it will take more time and effort, as well as create problems with the other passengers. It is only reasonable to surmise: If you go with the flow, you will achieve success more quickly, and with less opposition.

As you look to the seasonal changes or sabbats, keep the example of the escalator in mind. You want to work with the flow of the energy rather than oppose it. When you combine your personal energy with that of nature, you automatically enhance everything you do.

Working With the Sabbats

It is important to learn what the sabbats are all about before you try to work with them. You need to know what they mean on a physical, as well as spiritual, plane. Once their meanings are clear, then you can begin to correlate their significance with your needs. The following descriptions explain the meaning of each sabbat, its relationship to both the physical and spiritual plane, and its corresponding symbolism.

The Wheel of the Year: The Eight Witches' Sabbats

Yule/Winter Solstice

Yule is a pre-Christian holiday or festival which is celebrated on the Winter Solstice around December 21. It is the true New Year, both astronomically as well as spiritually. At this time, we see the simultaneous death and rebirth of the

Sun-God represented in the shortest day and longest night of the year. From this time forward, the sun grows in power and strength.

To our ancestors, from whom our teachings come, fertility was an important aspect of daily life. As the sun is vital to the concept of growth and fertility, it is only natural that its return was celebrated with elaborate rituals and ceremonies. Though we don't necessarily use the sabbat rites for fertility in a physical sense, the energy is still there and can be tapped.

Yule is the time to think about what you want to accomplish in the months to come. Now is the time to outline the goals you wish to work for. Write out your plan for the coming year on a small piece of paper. Place this in a hollow Christmas tree ornament along with allspice for wealth, rosemary for protection, cinnamon for success, and coriander for health. Tie red, green, and gold ribbons to the ornament and hang it above the door. When you have achieved your goals, take down the ornament and bury it in the ground.

Imbolc/Candlemas

Imbolc, also known as Oimele or Brigantia, is celebrated on February 1. This is the feast of the waxing light, or feast of lights, and is ascribed to the goddess Bridget, or Bride. This sabbat is associated with the return of life and light. Imbolc marks the awakening of the earth and the promise of spring; it is definitely a time of new beginnings.

In Greece, during the Eleusinian Mysteries, people held a torchlight procession on February 1 in honor of the goddess Demeter. The torch was to aid her in the search for her lost daughter Persephone. When she was found, light returned to the world. Celtic myths proclaimed this to be the time when the young lord god courted the virgin-maiden aspect of the Goddess. Their passion for each other is what melted the snow and returned the world to springtime. Closely related to Imbolc, the

Christian festival of Candlemas, celebrated on February 2, is a time of purification.

Imbolc is the time to prepare for what you wish to accomplish in the months to come. You should use this time to clarify and refine what you began at Yule. As this is a festival of lights, you will want to use a candle whose color, size, and shape best reflects your goal. If you make your own candle, add rose oil for love, cedar oil for courage, carnation oil for power, or lotus oil for healing. Inscribe your desire on the candle with your athame, and burn it daily to reaffirm and reflect its intended purpose.

Spring Equinox/Ostara

The Spring Equinox is celebrated around March 21. This is the time when the sun crosses the plane of the equator, making the day and night equal length. This is the actual beginning of spring and the agricultural season. In fact, most of our modern Easter customs come from the older Pagan Ostara or Spring Equinox celebrations. The most popular of these practices is that of decorating eggs. In ancient Egypt, Rome, Greece, and Persia, brightly colored eggs, symbolic of immortality, fertility, and resurrection, were eaten at this time.

The Spring Equinox is a time of balance, equality, and harmony between the masculine and feminine forces in nature. This is also the time when you physically, as well as symbolically, plant the seeds of your desires. The plants which grow from the seeds will represent what you are working for. When the plant bears fruit at harvest, so, too, should your desire manifest itself in physical form.

This is when you consummate the seeds of your desires by actually planting them. This is the first physical step in the process—to plant a seed which symbolically represents the outcome of your desire. Choose seeds which represent your projected goal. Use marigolds for prosperity and success, basil or coriander for love, thyme for health, and bittersweet for protection. Place your seeds in a plastic Easter egg or in a small basket tied with colored ribbon. Bless the seeds and then plant them when the weather permits.

Remember, what you decided to do at Yule and put into motion at Imbolc, you will be planting both physically and spiritually after the Vernal Equinox.

Beltane/May Eve

Beltane is celebrated on April 30 (May Eve) and is primarily a fire and fertility festival. Beltane, meaning "Bel-Fire," is derived from the Celtic god Bel, also known as Beli or Balor, which simply means "Lord." Some seem to think that Bel was comparable to the Celtic Gaul god, Cernunnos. This is possible, since most male gods relate to the sun and fire aspects.

Beltane is also the time of the May Queen, when a young woman was chosen from the village to represent the Earth Goddess and reflect the transformation of maiden to mother. This was also the time of the kindling of the Need Fire, when all fires in the village were extinguished and then ritually relit the following day.

Fertility played a significant role in Beltane celebrations. The principal symbol of this sabbat was the may pole, also known as the axis mundi, around which the universe revolved. The pole personified the thrusting masculine force, and the disk at the top depicted the receptive female. There were seven colored ribbons tied to it, which represented the seven colors of the rainbow. Fire and fertility, for the most part, dominated the rituals at Beltane.

At this time, we see the reaffirmation and union of energies; the movement toward the last half of the manifestation process. We have planted the seeds of desire, now we must reaffirm what we want as we energize the seeds. (Flowers tied with colorful ribbons, green plants, and the abundance of nature remind us of what we are working for.)

Summer Solstice/Midsummer

The Summer Solstice is celebrated around June 21 and is the longest day and shortest night of the year. The festival of the Summer Solstice is concerned with both fire and water, as from this point onward, the sun will decline in its power. The symbolism of fire was used in keeping the sun alive. The water element was used for the ritual blessing of individuals, sacred wells, and springs.

One of the customs of our ancestors was leaping over or passing through fires. It was believed that the higher they jumped, the higher the crops would grow. As with Beltane, cattle were driven through the fires for purification and fumigation. It was also believed that the fire repelled the powers of evil and would protect the cattle as well as all who passed through it.

Another symbol used at this time was the wheel. The turning of the wheel suggests the turning, or progression, of the seasons. Wheels were decorated with flowers and then lighted candles were placed on them. These were then taken to a body of water and set afloat. From the standpoint of symbolism and ritual, now is the time to nurture your goals or efforts. That which you have been working for should now be within range. You will want to continue to care for and sustain your impending goals in every way possible. Now is not the time to get careless or sloppy. On the other hand, being pushy or aggressive won't help either. Balance and steadfastness are the keys to success at Midsummer.

Because Midsummer is a celebration of both fire and water, you will need to express these concepts simultaneously. This can be easily accomplished by making what I call a water candle. Place a candle (the color of your desire) in a glass jar. Place this jar in another jar filled with water and a sprinkling of herbs (to give the water extra energy).

Add sassafras for health, orchid for love, lily of the valley for mental powers, or iris for wisdom. The water will be used to

water the plant which is growing from the seeds you planted at
the Vernal Equinox.

Lughnasadh/Lammas

The festival of Lughnasadh (Celtic) or Lammas (Christian) is
held on August 1. The word *Lughnasadh* is associated with the god
Lugh, and the festival was held to commemorate his marriage.
Lammas is derived from the Old English *hlafmoesse,* meaning "loaf-
mass," and was held in celebration of the first loaves baked from the
first grain harvested. The loaves were taken to the local church and
were then blessed by the priests. The loaves were then distributed
among the members of the congregation. Observing this festival
ensured an abundance of fruit and grain for the months to come.
The first fruit picked or sheaf cut was considered to be sacred to
the ancient gods, and was therefore treated in a special manner.

Corn and grain are the predominate features of rituals at this
time because they symbolize the fertility of the earth, the awakening of life, and life coming from death. The golden ears of
corn are seen as the offspring of the marriage of the sun and the
virgin earth. Corn and wine, like bread and wine, represent
humankind's labor and ability to sustain life.

Wine and candle-making were also important features of this
time of year, along with food-preserving and other preparations
for winter. Some customs included rush-bearing, decorating
water wells with vines, and the blessing of food.

This is the first harvest, and the time when you should be
accepting the responsibility as well as rewards for your labors.
Here you have the birth of your idea; your goal has begun to
actually physically manifest itself and now you must assume
responsibility for it. Just like the farmer who now has crops
which he or she can begin to harvest, so, too, do you have the
very beginnings of your goal in sight.

For this ritual, you will want to bless corn and freshly baked
bread. The corn will be used to make a corn baba for the

Autumnal Equinox, and the bread should be used for ritual feasting (continue reading for instructions for making a corn baba). Tie bundles of corn with red ribbons for strength and courage, yellow ribbons for intellectual prowess, green ribbons for wealth and prosperity, and blue ribbons for spiritual wisdom. Bake a loaf of bread and add some anise for protection, alfalfa for prosperity, and caraway for health.

Autumn Equinox/Mabon

The Autumnal Equinox, also known as Mabon, is celebrated sometime around September 21. Again, as with the spring Equinox, we have a time of equal day and night. However, after this night, the days grow shorter and the sun begins to wane in power.

This sabbat is also known as the Harvest Home and is basically the end of the agricultural year. Now all the crops have been gathered. Canning and storage for the winter is a priority, and wine-making is in full progress. Some things that come to mind are leaves turning color, bird migrations, corn harvesting, and bonfires.

The purpose of the Autumn Equinox is twofold: First, you want to give thanks for all you have received, second, you want to project for your ability to maintain what you possess. It does no good to manifest a goal if you cannot keep it. This is what the corn baba, which you will be making, represents: thanksgiving for what you have received, and request for the ability to keep what you have created. When constructing your corn baba,[1] bear

---

[1]To make a corn baba: Strip off dried husks from the corn cob and soak them in water until pliable. Use the cob as the body. Use paper, cotton, or a small Styrofoam ball for the head. Cover with strips of husks and attach them to the cob. Cut a narrow strip of husk, roll it into a seven-inch length, and tie it off at the ends, with a string for arms. Attach it to the cob and then fashion the dress from strips of corn husks, as in the picture. Use the silk or yellow yarn for hair. You may add a hat, basket, or other things which represent your objective: a dollar bill for prosperity, a heart for love, or a piece of paper with your desire written on it. There should be a larger version of the corn baba for your altar.

in mind what you have received and what you need to maintain. Bless your corn baba and then hang it above the main doorway in your home. Keep it until the next Autumn Equinox, when you will burn it and replace it with the new corn baba.

At this point, you should have what you are working for well within reach. Technically, your goal should have manifested itself by this time and you should be giving thanks for it.

Samhain/All Hallows Eve

Samhain, which means "end of the summer," is celebrated on October 31. It is the end of the agricultural season and the beginning of the Celtic New Year. Samhain is the festival of the dead and was christianized with the day that follows being designated All Soul's or All Saint's day. This is a time of chaos and the reversal of normal order; endings and beginnings are occurring simultaneously.

For our ancestors, Samhain was when the majority of the herd was butchered, providing food for the winter months. Slaughter, barren earth, and decreasing daylight made the concept of death an ever-present reality. Because of this, Samhain has always been considered a time when the veil between the worlds of the living and the dead was thin, a night of magick charms and divination, when the dead could be easily contacted.

On an individual basis, this is the time to rest and reevaluate your life and goals. Now is when you want to get rid of any negativity or opposition which may surround your achievements or hinder future progress. Samhain should have seen the accomplishment of your desires, and now you need to stabilize and protect what you have gained. This is important, since it is impossible to concentrate, let alone put energy into new goals, if what you have is not secure.

For this occasion you will want to prepare a protection bag. Write your desire on a small square of paper, place it into a black silk or cotton bag with stones for protection (onyx, black tourmaline, and obsidian), herbs for strength (bay, mulberry, and thistle), and something personal (a ring, a lock of hair, or photograph). Place the bag where it will do the most good. (Students can place the bag in their school locker, while those who travel can leave it in the car.)

The most important reason to celebrate the sabbats is to take advantage of the power emanating from the earth at these times. The planet's rotation, gravitational pull, and astrological configurations change with each season. Each season produces a different level of energy, which can be harnessed and channeled toward a specific intention. This is why it is best to create your own sabbat rites, so they will meet with your personal needs and energy levels.

Planning and creating a personal sabbat ritual can be a challenge. It does require time, research,[2] and imagination, but the end result is always worth the effort. I offer the following chart of correspondences, ritual outlines, and liturgy as a guide for designing your own special sabbat rite.

---

[2]For research, collect as many books as you can about Witchcraft, especially those which emphasize ritual work. Analyze each ritual in each book you have, and then compare them.

Sabbat	Meaning	Symbols	Offering	Color
Winter Solstice	Think	Yule log, evergreens, holly	Tree ornament filled with herbs and your wish	Red, green, silver, and gold
Imbolc	Prepare	Candles, snow, hearts, flowers	Candle to represent desire	White, pink, lilac, and pale blue
Vernal Equinox	Plant	Eggs, seeds, flower baskets	Seeds, hollow eggs filled with seeds	Pastel yellow, lavender, and green
Beltane	Act	Maypole, flowers, cauldron	Flower bundles tied with colored ribbons	Bright yellow, green, and white
Summer Solstice	Nurture	Wheel, cauldron, water, candles	Candles inside jars of colored water	Yellow, red, and white
Lughnasadh	Accept	Corn, grain, bread	Bundles of corn and fresh bread	Orange, yellow, and green
Autumnal Equinox	Receive	Corn baba, cornucopia, harvest foods	Corn baba	Orange, red, and brown
Samhain	Return	Skulls, horns, pumpkins, apples	Protection talisman	Black, red, and orange

The Basic Sabbat Rite

Mark off the ritual area with tape or chalk. Place your altar in the center of the circle and cover it with the appropriate colored cloth.[3] Decorate both the circle and the altar with seasonal symbols. Position your tools, two altar candles, cakes, wine, and accessories as usual. To represent the celebration of the sabbat, use a brightly colored candle set in a ring of seasonal flowers (see the sabbat correspondence chart for proper colors, symbols, and offerings).

The Opening

Consecrate the elements, cast the magick, and call in the guardians of the four quadrants in your usual manner.

Light the right altar candle and then the left altar candle as follows:

Right Candle:

> *Let this flame bring forth the light*
> *And grant to me power and might.*

Left Candle:

> *Let this flame bless my sabbat rite*
> *And grant to me wisdom and insight.*

The Minor Invocation

Light the incense, hold it in offering, and say with great feeling and elation:

---

[3]An appropriate colored cloth is a cloth that will match the color of the season: white, Winter Solstice; pink, Imbolc; lilac, Spring Equinox; green, Beltane; yellow, Summer Solstice; orange, Lughnasadh; red, Autumnal Equinox; and black, Samhain.

Source of Great Mystery
Whose secrets are in the Air
On this sabbat night
Do I your rapture share.

The Major Invocation

Light the sabbat candle and hold it in offering as you speak with great conviction:

Eternal Source, my prayer now hear
Greatest of Forces, whom I revere.
Endow me with your power strong
For this is what I crave and long.
In your crowning light I stand
And only ask you lend a hand
To help me learn and see the way
And grant me happiness from this day!

The Petition

Now offer the sabbat candle to each of the quadrants. Speak the following petitions as you offer the candle:

East

I beseech the East, the home of moonlight and consciousness, to endow me with great wisdom.

South

I beseech the South, the home of fire and inspiration, to endow me with great strength.

West

I beseech the West, the home of my watery beginning, to endow me with great understanding.

North

> *I beseech the North, the home of all that is green and*
> *fruitful, to endow me with great ability.*

The Offering

Sprinkle some salt and water on your offering. Now pass the offering through the flame of the sabbat candle and smoke of the incense. Say the following blessing on your offering:

> *Hail exalted Source of celestial power*
> *Whose sovereignty reigns from above*
> *Be with me in this sabbat hour*
> *And bless this offering with your love.*

The Meditation

This is your own personal time to meditate and reflect on the meaning of the sabbat. Use this time to think about the meaning of the sabbat and what you want to accomplish in the coming months. Make your own prayers and petitions at this time.

The Consecration of the Cakes and Wine

Place your left hand over the chalice filled with wine and your right hand over the plate of cakes. Feel the force be with you as you ask the following blessing:

> *I bless thee with courage and wisdom*
> *I bless thee with strength and might*
> *I bless thee with warmth and pleasure*
> *I bless thee with love and light*
> *So Mote It Be.*

Drink the wine and eat the cakes in honor of the occasion. Of course, if you are working with a specific god or goddess at this time, you will want to drink and eat in their honor.

The Closing

Dismiss the guardians, beginning with the North and working in a Widdershins manner.

Extinguish the altar candles as follows:

Left:

> *Let now the flame of this sabbat rite*
> *Return unto the original light.*

Right:

> *Let now the potential, power, and force*
> *Return unto the original source.*

Banish the Circle

The sabbat candle is left to burn out. If it is a large candle and will take several days to burn out, then you can put it in a coffee can to protect it from being knocked over or blown out.

Thoughts and Ideas

As you look at the meaning of each sabbat, a pattern appears. This pattern is one of a logical progression through each of the seasonal changes. When looked at separately, each one of these points in time is unique and special. However, when viewed collectively and in relation to each other, they provide the ideal situation for beginning and ending magickal operations.

Magick is about making things happen the way you want them to. It is about combining what is at hand, or already exists, with the energy of a specific desire. When this is done, a special dynamic[4] is created and the process of the manifestation cycle is completed. This may sound confusing, but in reality it is

---

[4]Dynamic: potential energy in a state of conversion; the opposite of statis; the potential of the human being and consciousness.

very simple. For once you begin to incorporate the natural energy of the universe into your daily life, magick becomes almost second nature. Things just seem to happen the way you want them to.

Most of what I am saying will become apparent when you begin to work with the seasonal energies. By focusing your energy on the sabbats, you come into alignment with the seasonal vibrations of the universe. These vibrations or energies help to push your desires through their various stages of development. From planning through planting to harvest, you have the powers of nature working with you, adding strength and energy to your personal magickal operations.

The sabbats also provide you with a natural timeframe in which to work and measure your progress. In short, using the sabbats as a formula for success is very simple. First you will think about what you want to do or accomplish at Yule; then write this down and make a talisman to represent the idea (see Chapter 14). At Imbolc, you will begin to prepare for the accomplishment of your goal. You will use a candle as your focal point. When the Spring Equinox arrives, it is time to actually plant the seeds of your desire. This is done by energizing and planting seeds that will grow, giving symbolic life in physical form to your goals. During Beltane and the Summer Solstice, you will nurture both your plant and your desire with specially energized water, the water being symbolic of the life-giving and nurturing energy of the Earth Mother. By the time Lughnasadh has arrived, you should be ready to accept the responsibility for your goal by blessing corn and bread at the first harvest. At the Autumn Equinox, you should have received your desire and be ready to give thanks for your bounty. Samhain is the time you will want to return and release any negativity which may surround your newly acquired objectives so you can stabilize yourself and begin again with something new.

9

Magickal Ritual Methods

Indubitably, Magic is one of the subtlest and most difficult of the sciences and arts. There is more opportunity
for errors of comprehension, judgement, and practice
than in any other branch of physics.

—Alister Crowley (1875-1947) British occultist

This book, or any other for that matter, is worth little if you are
not willing to apply its knowledge to your present situation. Pure
and simple, we are all physical beings attached to a material
world. If we want to be successful, we must react to our environment in a rational manner, mainly because logic values the
system in which it retains its own momentum. Magick, through
the use of imaginary symbolic tools and ritual, helps the individual realign with the natural forces and energies of the universe. In return, this alignment will bring about change, growth,
progress, and inner harmony.

"What the mind can imagine, the will can create" should be
every aspiring Witch's motto. The only thing standing in your way

or keeping you from getting what you want is your inability to manifest your thoughts. However, this can be changed through the use of Witchcraft and ritual magick.

The easiest and most efficient way to enter into ritual magick is by becoming aware of the natural forces which surround us. By aligning ourselves with natural forces and becoming aware of cycles and changes in our environment, we begin to move with the flow of the universe. Once we are caught up in this current of universal movement, it is only natural to feel its power. We begin to feel connected to, rather than separated from, that which surrounds us.

For magickal purposes, it is imperative to be able to relate to our surroundings. We must be able to feel the energy flowing through us, combining our individual power with that which already exists. It is only reasonable to take advantage of what is here and now, as this simplifies the entire creation process and speeds up the time involved in manifesting a desire.

Just What Is a Ritual?

A ritual is a prescribed event or particular ceremony that is built up by tradition and carries with it a great amount of energy, light, force, and impact. Atmosphere, dress, and symbology contribute to the event, as does the use of repetitious activity. The key to effective ritual magick is repetitious activity. By this, I mean doing the exact same thing, in the exact same way, each and every time. This single point cannot be stressed enough. Spontaneous ritual is fun, but repetitious ritual is effective.

What is Ritual Magick?

Ritual magick is the creation of a specific ceremony (using repetitious activity in a controlled environment) to cause or force a change to occur in accordance with your will. The only reason for doing ritual magick is to change something, even if the change is only one of personal attitude.

Everything in this universe is in a constant state of change, and as we are part and party to the universal consciousness, we must learn to go with the flow or be swept away by its momentum. If you are going to do magick, you must be willing to accept the unavoidable process of change. It is only when you change your attitude, outlook, and way of thinking that things around you begin to change as well.

Change can be frightening to the poor ego.[1] This is especially true when one begins to dabble in Witchcraft and the magickal arts. Once the higher self begins to see the possibilities, it will no longer tolerate excuses as to why it doesn't have what is wanted and needed. This is something to consider before you get involved in magick. The higher self will tolerate ignorance but not laziness.

WORKING WITH RITUAL MAGICK

There are three reasons for performing ritual:

- Spiritual—to spiritually align oneself with a specific divine energy source, such as an archangel.

- Religious—to celebrate a specific day or time of power, i.e., full moons, sabbats, the new year, harvest time, and so forth.

- Material—to create or manifest a desired goal for the purpose of obtaining something on the material plane. This could be anything from getting a raise in pay to healing a consenting injured friend.

---

[1]Ego is the conditioned motivating force which was formed outside of our own determined will; it is that which projects, protects, and receives information for the true identity, or soul essence, of the individual. It is the mask you wear for others to see.

It is important that your motives or intentions are clear, for they will greatly influence your productivity during ritual. The higher self knows why you are doing something even when you try to pretend otherwise. Be totally honest about your intentions, especially with yourself. Your reasons are your own and perfectly justifiable if approached in a sincere manner. The point of doing any ritual is to create a flow of energy, not engage in battle with your higher consciousness.

Ritual Design

Once you have considered the reason for performing the ritual and decided upon a theme, you need to write the ceremony itself. When preparing any ritual, there are four distinct segments with which you must deal if the ritual is to be effective. All four of these segments must combine effortlessly in order for the ritual to flow smoothly.

One: Preparation and Consecration

The first segment is preparation and consecration. This is important, as it sets the tone and mood of the ritual. In this first part, we will consider the physical setting of the ritual area. Make a list of all the items that will be needed and note their proper position. While you are setting up, you will actually be creating sacred space. This is done by the consecration and casting of the magick circle, which creates a boundary between you and the physical world. The casting of the circle and calling in of the Guardians is the actual beginning of your ceremony. This should all be performed with great respect and reverence.

Once the circle has been cast and the Guardians called in, the altar candles are lit. It is at this point that you will invoke your god or goddess if you are working with deity.

Two: Petition and Honor

The next step in the ritual procedure is that of the petition. The petition describes in one form or another the reason for doing the ritual. It may be a story, a descriptive poem, or just a simple prayer to a deity. The most important aspect of the petition is the statement of the petitioner's desire. During this segment of the ritual, drumming, dancing, or chanting may be used to raise energy for the petition. Chanting is the intoning of a chosen sound or rhythmic poem to accomplish a definite purpose. Chants are repetitive and are usually spoken in a monotone with varying degrees of intensity. The rhythm of the chant and its intensity causes the energy level within the circle to rise. This energy is then directed toward the desired goal.

Three: Offering and Blessing

This is the time when symbolic offerings[2] are made. These are usually made to enhance the consideration of the ritual petitions or are remembrances of something special which has been received. This is also the stage of ritual when the blessing of the cakes and wine[3] is performed. The blessing, and then the partaking of the wine and cakes, usually signals the conclusion of the working part of the ritual. Most Witches use this time to reflect or meditate on the ritual.

---

[2]Symbolic Offerings: these are usually in the form of flowers, incense, smudge, or food, which gives life energy or power to enhance or heighten the level of energy being produced by the petitions. A good example would be offering corn to a god or goddess to thank them for something they have given us, or using incense to be sure our message or petition drifted in a heavenly direction.

[3]Blessing of cakes and wine: hold your hands over the wine and ask a simple blessing, "I bless thee with warmth and pleasure, I bless thee with love and light. So mote it be." Repeat the blessing over the cakes.

Four: Closing and Dismissal

At this time the ceremony is brought to an end, and all of the energies raised in the circle are banished. This is important because raised energy needs to be let go in order to be able to work. Another reason for getting rid of the raised energy is that you don't want it to interfere with other projects which may be at cross purposes with each other.

The ending of a ritual is very much like its beginning. There are certain steps which must be taken and things which must be done in order to ensure the proper release of energy. If you took the time to build a proper circle, then you will need to take the same amount of time to disassemble it.

Well-defined ritual closure is just as important as proper preparation and consecration. All you need to do is retrace your opening steps, only this time in reverse order. Begin by extinguishing the altar candles, then dismiss the Guardians, and take down, or disassemble, the circle of power.

Whenever you write a ritual, it is a good idea to keep the above instructions in mind. These suggestions will help you format your ceremonies in an organized manner so they will present a clear purpose and flow smoothly.

Ritual Transcript

Next to be considered is the ritual transcript. This should express in written form the totality of your intent, as well as what you will need to bring it about. All transcripts of ritual, as well as accounts of magickal works, should be kept in your Book of Shadows for future reference.

Below, I have provided you with the basic framework for creating a ritual transcript. Copy the categories, in the order they appear, onto a blank sheet of paper. Use this form as a guideline when preparing your rituals and magickal works.

1. Category of ritual: *(Is the ritual spiritual, religious, or material?)* _____

2. Date and time: *(When will the ritual take place? This should include the phase of the moon, planetary considerations, and the physical setting of the ritual.)* _____

3. Desire and intent: *(What is it that you want? For what reasons are you going to do the ritual? Be honest, because this will add drive and energy to your work. Don't be afraid to write down what you want. If you are too embarrassed to put your desires into writing because you feel they are unworthy, then you should not attempt to bring them into manifestation.)* _____

_____

_____

4. Tools and symbols: *(List all the tools, symbols, and items you will be using for the ritual. Include things like charcoal, matches, salt, and water.)* _____

_____

_____

5. Ritual composition: *(Put your ritual in writing. Each and every word, action, or expression, from consecration to dismantling, should be written down.)* _____

_____

_____

_____

_____

_____

_____

6. Physical perception: *(As soon as you have finished with the ritual, write down what happened. Explain the physical sensations you felt during the ceremony. If anything significant happened, be sure to write it down, as it could be of importance later on.)* _____

_____

_____

7. Results: *(Keep an accurate record of the results of your magickal works. If what you were working for manifested as intended, then be sure to write down when and how it came to be. If, on the other hand, your desire did not come to fruition, be sure to make note of that as well. Retrospect commentary is the only way you have of proving and improving your magickal abilities.)* _____

_____

_____

_____

_____

Thoughts and Ideas

A ritual is like a play because it expresses an idea or concept in material form. A properly performed ritual will make an impression on its surrounding atmosphere and on the consciousness of the individuals involved. Ritual should always have a purpose and be enjoyable, not something you do because there is nothing good on television. If you are going to do a ritual, do it correctly and with an objective in mind. Follow proper procedure, prepare yourself in advance, and your rituals will work.

Many things go into a ritual to make it work. Attention to proper symbolism, atmosphere, and ritual attire should be taken into consideration long before the event is to take place. It is also a good idea to rehearse the ritual several times before you do it. By doing this, everyone who plans to participate will know what they should be doing in advance.

Another good thing to remember when constructing or performing ritual is to "only ask for what you need, and you will ever abound." Ritual magick is a tool, and when properly used it will be of benefit to all concerned. Because ritual magick is a tool, it is controlled solely by the individual wielding it. No matter what kind of magick you are doing, its final results and ramifications are your responsibility. Therefore, it behooves you to think carefully before you engage in any magickal act.

10

Foreseeing the Future

> We should all be concerned about the future because we will have to spend the rest of our lives there.
>
> —C.F. Kettering (1876–1958) American industrialist

Everyone has wondered, at some point, what the future holds. In fact, the lure of the unknown is a distinctive characteristic of human beings. For the most part, we all base our choices on the potential outcome of what we foresee. Our desire to know makes the science of prediction an indispensable art, as well as a profitable occupation, for those who can master it.

The reputable fortune-teller, seer, or psychic has always played a significant role in world history and culture. The oracles of ancient Greece, biblical prophecies, and modern fortune-tellers are testaments to humankind's "need to know" fixation. Even in our "enlightened" times, some people can't start the day without reading their horoscope or consulting their 1-900 number psychic. Times may have changed, but human nature has stayed the same—human beings want to know before they act.

Divination

Divination can best be described as the prediction of the future or the discovery of secrets by means of a variety of occult[1] methods. The *Encyclopedic Psychic Dictionary* (1986, by June Bletzer, the Donning Co./Publishers, Norfolk, VA), describes divination as a "gift from the divine," information received from God; the ability to receive this information (the gift) is acquired through one's own initiative. The Larousse *Dictionary of Beliefs & Religion* explains divination to be a method used to gain information about people, phenomena, or the future by means not amenable to normal investigation. Basically, divination is a process used to point out obstacles or situations so they can be dealt with before they become problems.

How many times have you said to yourself, or heard someone say, "if I had only known, I would have done things differently." Of course you would have done things differently, we would all do things differently if we could see the ramifications of our actions in advance. This is why divination is such an important part of Witchcraft. It allows the Witch to anticipate what will happen in advance, thus avoiding the pitfalls which plague most non-Witches.

The principal force behind divination is mentality, the extension of time through which the mind is allowed to express itself. The extension of time and expression of the mind can best be explained as "inner film stills," which can be viewed by the individual at any given point. Theoretically, there is no time or space for the unconscious mind, which is the vehicle of divination. The past, present, and future are all open to the scrutiny of that deep unconscious intelligence which lies within us all.

Mystics have long held that all the knowledge of the past, present, and future is locked and carefully safeguarded in a secret compartment of the brain. The information stored in this compartment

---

[1] The word *occult* refers to "hidden" or "secret," meaning the act is held in private by the individual using it.

is available to the conscious mind. All any individual has to do is find the key that will open the compartment. It is believed that the key which will unlock this secret compartment is contained in the many, and various, systems of divination. It is up to the individual to discover which system holds the key that will unlock his or her compartment.

There are innumerable ways to divine the future, and it would take a set of encyclopedias to do them all justice. Some of the more traditional forms of divination are described here. Following these general descriptions are complete instructions for working with cards, Runes, and tea leaves. As with all Witchcraft, it is really up to the individual to explore and experiment until the right system is found.

Standard Forms of Divination

Austromancy: Fortune-telling by the study of winds. The effects of wind on bells hanging in a tree or ripples on a pond are noted and interpreted.

Bibliomancy: Seeking advice through the random choice of words in a book. Any book will do, but the Bible is usually the book of choice. Close your eyes, open the book to any page, and the first words you read will provide the answer to the problem.

Cartomancy: Fortune-telling with playing cards. Specifically designed Tarot cards are usually the choice of the reader, but regular playing cards can also be used. Each card is assigned a symbolic meaning. How the cards appear in relationship to each other determine the final outcome.

Ceromancy: Divination from the patterns of melted wax dropped into a dish of cold water.

Crystallomancy: The practice of gazing into a crystal, usually referred to as scrying. The diviner gazes into a crystal ball, or bowl of water, and interprets the images which are revealed in it. For example, a rabbit or frog indicates fertility, a dark cloud indicates danger or death, and a boat or car indicates travel.

Geomancy: Divination of marks made in a box of earth. Theoretically, geomancy is carried out by the diviner in collaboration with the gnomes, or elemental spirits of the earth.

Lithomancy: Fortune-telling with precious or semiprecious stones. Stones are picked from a bag and each carry a different symbolic meaning. A ruby or red stone, indicates romance, an amethyst or purple stone signifies family problems.

Numerology or Arithomancy: Fortune-telling by numbers. Letters in the name are given numerical value, or the numbers in a birth date are used to produce a personal number, giving an indication of personality.

Runes: Divination through the use of stones or ceramic cubes inscribed with the mystical Germanic alphabet. The symbols on the stones are interpreted according to predetermined corresponding meanings.

Tasseography: Fortune-telling with tea leaves. Loose tea is placed in a cup of water, stirred, and the water is poured out. The patterns made by the remaining tea leaves are then interpreted.

WORKING WITH DIVINATION

Cartomancy

Cartomancy, or card reading, is one of the most popular forms of divination used today. Because our modern playing cards evolved from the ancient Tarot deck, they are very symbolic and mystical. For example, the fifty-two cards in a typical deck correspond to the number of weeks in a year. The four suits align with the number of weeks in a month, the four elements, and the number of seasons in a year. Half the pack is red and the other half is black. This symbolizes the male and female, light and dark, good and bad, forces within the structure of the universe.

Each card in the deck has an accepted meaning attached to it, as well as a reversed meaning. When a card appears in a spread upside down this is referred to as reversed, and the meaning is consequently modified, or in some cases negated.

All cards were originally designed to be viewed from one direction, just as the Tarot cards still are. Unfortunately, most modern decks of playing cards are made to be viewed from either way. This accounts for their individual significance being placed in the top left, as well as bottom right, corners. If this is the type of deck you have, you must mark the cards to indicate which end is going to represent up.

To mark the cards, place a pencil or ink mark in the center of the top edge of each card. This will serve to distinguish right-side up from reverse. You can also mark your cards by placing one word, which signifies the basic meaning of the card, on the top edge instead of the plain mark. For example, you would mark the edge of the Eight of Hearts with the word *love*, this would then denote the direction of the card as well as its meaning.

Once you have chosen a deck and marked it, the cards should only be used for reading. It is also advisable to keep your cards wrapped in a silk scarf. Pure silk will protect them from outside vibrations when they are not being used. Choose a solid color which is conducive to higher thought such as purple, gold, or royal blue. Treat your cards with respect, as you would any other magickal tool, and they will serve you well.

Card Interpretations

The following meanings have traditionally been assigned to each of the fifty-two cards in an ordinary deck. It is best to memorize the definitions before you attempt to read for other people. I suggest you keep two packs of cards, one marked with the meanings on each card and the other left plain. Once you memorize the meanings of the cards, you can then switch to the unmarked deck when reading for friends or clients.

Hearts are considered lucky. They represent your emotions, friendships, love, marriage, and domestic life. They can also stand for ambitions successfully realized.

Ace: Love letter, good news, your home, new love. Reversed: Disappointment, a visit from a friend.

Two: You will attend a wedding or funeral. Reversed: A short spell of loneliness.

Three: A new admirer, love on the way. Reversed: An unwanted communication.

Four: To the single, marriage; to the married, a confirmation of commitment. Reversed: Emotional turmoil is possible.

Five: A pleasant surprise. Reversed: Could mean bad news.

Six: Children and their world. Reversed: A desire for more space.

Seven: Contentment and favors. Reversed: Disappointment in love, jealousy, boredom.

Eight: Love and romance, invitations. Reversed: Unreciprocated affections, jealousy.

Nine: The "wish card," success, a christening. Reversed: Passing troubles.

Ten: More good fortune, great happiness, success in love. Reversed: Changes, a birth, a loss.

Jack: A fair young man, pleasure loving, a bachelor, friend, or lover. Reversed: A lover with problems, grievance, a playboy.

Queen: A fair woman, generous and loving, sensual. Reversed: Crossed in love, unsympathetic, capricious.

King: A fair man, kindhearted, giving, loving. Reversed: Uncertain, cold, inconstant lover.

Diamonds influence life outside and away from the home. They also suggest ambitions and money which must be gained through hard work.

Ace: A ring or money, new beginnings. Reversed: Demand for a debt, bad news.

Two: Sharp words, arguments, problems with money. Reversed: Think, put others before yourself.

Three: A time to meet with an old friend. Reversed: Time for reflection, use caution.

Four: An event causing rage, anger, hostility. Reversed: Sudden enlightenment, you know what to do.

Five: A settlement of troubles, things work out. Reversed: Beware of causing jealousy, someone is envious.

Six: A visitor is coming. Reversed: Must learn to control your temper.

Seven: Financial loss, friends criticize your efforts. Reversed: Scandal; there may be a minor success.

Eight: Short journey, a time for new clothes, love may be coming. Reversed: Your affections are being ignored.

Nine: Some anxiety, financial prosperity, news. Reversed: Danger, beware of family quarrels.

Ten: Legal matters, keep an eye on financial matters, a journey. Reversed: Misfortune and disappointment.

Jack: An official or messenger, a fair young man. Reversed: Wrongdoing, troublemaker.

Queen: A widow, someone will gossip, a fair young woman. Reversed: Flirt, not to be trusted.

King: A widower, a fair or graying man, could be deceitful. Reversed: A cunning man, not to be trusted, treachery.

Spades warn of problems, suffering, and misfortune. Beware of treachery, deceit, and enemies. Spades suggest danger and a time to be alert.

Ace: Satisfaction in love, high buildings. Reversed: Death of a relative, misfortune, illness.

Two: You may attend a funeral. Reversed: Static, dull period, boredom.

Three: Tears, a time of mourning, regret. Reversed: Light at the end of the tunnel, things will work out.

Four: You will visit with a sick friend, understanding. Reversed: Better news is on the way, be alert.

Five: A pleasant surprise awaits you. Reversed: Be careful, plan ahead, keep alert.

Six: A plan will fail, unexpected threats. Reversed: Try not to get too discouraged, chin up.

Seven: A move is evident, a resolution is close by. Reversed: There could be an accident or loss.

Eight: Sorrow, unwelcome visitor, illness. Reversed: Quarrels, rejected affection, negativity.

Nine: Disappointment, financial or domestic difficulties. Reversed: Death of a friend or loved one.

Ten: Grief, voyage across water, displacement. Reversed: Time of ill health, minor sickness.

Jack: A bad-mannered dark young man, lawyer, or doctor. Reversed: A traitor, he will deceive you.

Queen: A dark young woman, a friend, a widow. Reversed: This person could be treacherous.

King: A widower, untrustworthy, a dark man, lawyer. Reversed: A very dangerous man, evil, not to be trusted.

Clubs are the cards of success and are connected with money, business, and loyalty. However, they can also be associated with financial problems, failure, betrayal.

Ace: A temporary boost to income, a letter, news. Reversed: Possible bad news, delay in financial reward.

Two: Unnecessary worry over financial matters, stay calm. Reversed: Beware of a false friend.

Three: A friend will help with financial matters. Reversed: Struggle and difficult times ahead.

Four: An unfamiliar place or house. Reversed: A friend's intentions not clear.

Five: A package will arrive. Reversed: Time to take extra care of financial matters.

Six: Urgent and unexpected news. Reversed: Be careful not to tread on other people's toes.

Seven: Success with finances. Reversed: There could be a loss or an accident.

Eight: Changes, love of a dark man or woman, good luck. Reversed: Litigation, trouble, documents cause problems.

Nine: A legacy or a gathering of friends. Reversed: Beware of obstacles.

Ten: A sudden large sum of money, a journey. Reversed: Alienation, a journey over water.

Jack: A good lover and clever young dark man. Reversed: Your luck may change.

Queen: A very affectionate, young or old, dark woman. Reversed: A social climber, lives off others, not to be trusted.

King: Financial status important, a dark man, friendly and straightforward. Reversed: Worries and some problems ahead.

Playing-Card Layout Patterns

The real art of card reading lies in being able to blend the meanings of the cards into a cohesive story. Each card, like each word in a sentence, has a specific meaning. When you put them together, just as you do the words in a sentence, you end up with a meaningful story. The trick is to be able to interpret the whole picture by allowing each card to influence its neighboring card.

Here are a few examples of how the cards influence each other. Two Queens together signify gossip, two or more Aces imply surprising events, and a combination of twos alert to a possible plot. Color can also play an important role in your reading. An abundance of black cards indicates difficult problems in the past, whereas a predominance of red cards means the reverse.

The Seven-Pointed Star Spread: This spread allows you to get an overview of the week ahead. Shuffle the cards seven times and cut the deck. From the top of the deck, deal seven cards in the pattern indicated below. Turn the top right card over first. Working clockwise, turn each card over and read according to the instructions below.

The first card represents Sunday, the second Monday, and so on. (You can, of course, start with whatever day you happen to read the cards). You can read each card separately as an indication of the day's events, or you can read the cards as a progression of events.

Look for immediate indications of direction. An abundance of hearts signifies love interests or emotions, a majority of face cards may point to problems with friends, coworkers, or relatives. If there is an abundance of black cards, there may be an unresolved problem from the past which needs attention.

The most important thing is to be objective. Look at each card and think about what it means to you. Try to place the card in the situation you are examining. Endeavor to incorporate its symbolism into a solution, or answer, for the problem at hand. Most importantly, be open and listen to that little voice inside.

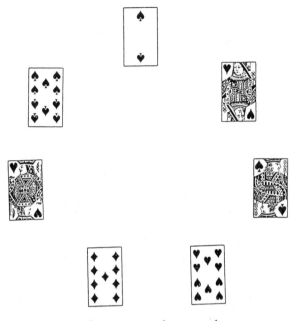

The seven-pointed star spread

The Six-Card Spread: The six-card spread is used to obtain a
yes or no answer to a direct question. Once the answer has been
determined, further interpretation of the cards will reveal the
proper course of action to take. As with most detailed readings,
the six-card spread will provide you with a choice regarding the
future, and its ultimate outcome.

Shuffle the cards several times, this helps to remove old vibrations and implant new ones. As you shuffle the cards, concentrate
on your question. When you feel the cards have been thoroughly
shuffled, place them on the table in front of you. Spread out the
cards face down and pull six from the deck. Lay these cards in a
row in the order you pulled them, and then turn them over.
Begin with the card to your left. (See the diagram below.)

First, look to see how many cards are right-side up or
reversed. If four or more cards are right-side up, then the answer

The six-card spread

to your question is yes. If four or more of the cards are reversed, then the answer is no. If the cards are equally divided, with three up and three reversed, the answer is uncertain at this time. You would do well to wait and ask again later.

For more information regarding the answer you received, read the value of the cards according to the spread pattern. The first two cards on the left represent the immediate past, or what has happened in the last thirty days. These cards indicate those vibrations which are just passing away. Remember, the past is always responsible for the present.

Now look at the two middle cards. They indicate the present circumstances which surround you at this time. Read these cards in conjunction with the two past cards; this will provide insight regarding the next two cards. These last two cards are the future cards, and indicate what the outcome will be based on the past and present circumstances revealed through the other cards. It is helpful to remember that the past has direct influence on the present, and the present is what will shape the future. When you do a reading, keep in mind that the cards do not render an absolute decision, but rather an alternative resolution to the situation inquired about.

Tasseography (Tea Leaf Reading)

Tea leaf reading, or tasseography, belongs to the vast range of divination methods involving the interpretation of images or symbols. It is both simple and entertaining, and depends a great deal on the imagination of the diviner. Because it only requires a cup

1. Rim—Present

2. Halfway—Near future

3. Bottom—Distant future

4. Handle—House and Querist

5. Left side—Something coming

6. Right side—Something departing

The stations of the cup

and some good loose tea, tasseography can be performed just about anywhere.

To read tea leaves, use a clean white cup with a wide top, slanted sides, and an unridged bottom surface. Use a good brand of Chinese tea which has a minimum of tea dust. Brew the tea in a teapot without a strainer, and allow a sufficient amount of leaves to flow with the water into the cup.

The person whose fortune is to be read should drink the tea, leaving a little in the bottom of the cup. Once a sufficient amount of tea has been consumed the querist will swirl the dregs in the bottom of the cup three times and then turn the cup upside down on a saucer to drain off the remaining liquid. This action will distribute the tea leaves around the sides of the cup, with some reaching the rim, while still leaving some on the bottom.

The patterns the leaves make on the various parts of the cup is what determines the fortune of the individual. The rim of the cup represents the present, or next few days. The sides of the cup represent the future, and the bottom the very distant future. The handle area of the cup is referred to as the house, and represents the querist. It is the immediate area, or scope, of the surrounding vibrations. The closer a symbol is to the house, or handle, the sooner the event will take place.

The images and symbols which appear in the cup are then classified into categories. Numbers signify people, days, weeks, or even amounts of money. Letters refer to people or initials of locations. Clear symbols are very lucky and denote positive circumstances, while poorly lined symbols indicate uncertainty. Clearly defined stars and triangles are good fortune; circles, success; and squares signify protection. Straight lines indicate a plan which should be followed, while wavy lines mean uncertainty.

Tea Leaf Symbols and Their Meanings

Acorn: Top: wealth; middle: health; bottom: happiness.

Airplane: Sudden journey, new project.

Alligator: Treachery lies in wait.

Anchor: Near top: success in business. If near middle: voyage ending in prosperity. If near bottom: good fortune socially.

Airplane

Ants: Persistence will succeed.

Anvil: Keep persisting.

Apple: Success.

Ant

Arch: Unexpected happening.

Arrow: Bad news is coming.

Axe: Danger.

Baby: New interests or addition to family.

Bag: A waiting trap.

Ball: Restlessness.

Baby

Basket: Useful gift. If at handle: baby. If at top: more worldly possessions. Filled with flowers: happiness and success.

Bat: Fear of authority; false friends.

Bear: Misfortune because of not thinking.

Bed: Laziness or neatness depending on look of symbol. (If the image of the bed appears clearly, it can be interpreted as neatness).

Bee: Good news; plural: a busy time ahead.
Bell: Promotion; happy union; two: great joy.
Birds: Good news and good luck.
Bird cage: Confinement and frustration.
Boat: Desire for travel.
Book: New information.
Boot: New home.
Bottle: Illness.
Bouquet: Happiness.
Box: Uncertainty.
Bracelet: A gathering of friends.
Broom: New beginnings.
Building: Desire for a new home or job.
Bull: Quarreling ahead.
Butterfly: Pleasure and fun soon.
Cabbage: Envy.
Cage: Proposal.
Candle: Educational want or zeal.
Car: Change of surroundings.
Castle: A wish to be fulfilled; strong character.
Cat: False friends, deceit.
Chain: News of a marriage.
Chair: Time to relax.
Chicken: Ability.
Child: Innocence.
Church: Faith.
Circle: A successful outcome.
Clock: Illness.
Clouds: Problems and doubts.
Clover: Luck.
Clown: Simple pleasures.
Coffin: Failure, bad news, perhaps death.
Comet: Unexpected happenings, an overseas visitor.
Compass: Travel.

Bee

Broom

Candle

Cat

Clover

Cow: Prosperity.

Crab: Interference.

Cradle: Children.

Cross: Suffering, sacrifice; two: a major affliction.

Cross

Crow: Trouble coming.

Crown: Success, probably because of luck.

Cymbal: Caution!

Cup: Happiness or a new friend.

Daffodil: Success, wealth, hope.

Dagger: Danger from enemies.

Dagger

Daisy: Simplicity; easy love.

Deer: Be careful of arguments.

Dog: True friendship. Seen running: good news. If at bottom: friend in trouble.

Dog

Donkey: Patience.

Door: Unexpected and unusual event.

Dot: Single: emphasizes nearest symbol. In groups: money.

Dove: Messenger of love.

Dragon: New beginning.

Drum: Time for change; scandal threatens.

Duck: Persistence in finance needed.

Eagle: Fame.

Ear: Pleasant news.

Earring: Luxury coming.

Easel: Chance to learn a new skill.

Egg: Good luck.

Elephant: Assistance to be remembered; solid success.

Eye: Watch for opportunity, especially in business.

Eye

Face: Friends.

Fairy: Romance coming.

Fan: Flirtations.

Feather: Fantastic good luck.
Fence: Limitations on plans.
Fern: Restlessness; unfaithfulness in lover.
Fire: Avoid danger.
Fish: Gambling luck.
Flag: Trouble ahead.
Flies: Petty annoyances.
Flower: Token of love.
Fountain: Everlasting love.
Fruit: Ambition satisfied; luck.
Gate: Problems.
Glasses: Caution needed; integrity.
Goat: Stubborn enemies threaten.
Grass: Ease and luxury.
Gun: Avoid quarrels. If near handle: domestic. If at bottom: business.
Hammer: Reward soon because of hard work.
Hand: Help from a friend.
Hare: Sadness, timidity.
Harp: Romance.
Hat: Fame.
Heart: Love and happiness.
Hill: Obstacle to progress.
Hive: Future prosperity.
Horn: Abundance.
Horse: Just its head: a lover. If running: good news.
Horseshoe: Good luck.
Hourglass: Decisions.
House: Success.
Initials: People you will know or know now.
Inkwell: Letter with good news.
Insect: Minor worries will be overcome.
Ivy: True love.
Jewel: A legacy.

Feather

Fire

Fish

Glasses

Gun

Horn

Hourglass

Jockey: Gambling.

Jug: Extravagance.

Kettle: Home comforts. If at bottom: domestic strife.

Kettle

Key: An advantage coming.

Kite: High ambition will succeed with persistence.

Knife: Illness, separation, arguments.

Ladder: Success, prosperity.

Lamp: Celebrations.

Ladder

Leaf: A letter. Many: hope, lovers.

Letters: News.

Lion: Influential friends.

Loaf: Domestic happiness.

Lock: Obstacles.

Leaf

Man: Visitor. Seen with outstretched arm: bearing gifts.

Mask: Insincerity.

Mermaid: Temptation.

Miter: Deserved fame.

Monkey: Flatterers and mischief.

Moon: Romance coming.

Moon

Mountain: Difficulties ahead.

Mouse: Theft.

Mushroom: Mental or physical disturbance.

Nail: Pain, malice threatens.

Necklace: Success. Seen broken: marriage or love broken.

Nail

Needle: Trouble, then joy!

Net: Beware! Traps ahead!

Nose: Great discovery.

Nun: Confinement.

Nurse: Illness.

Numbers: Time, days or weeks.

Oak: Long life.

Owl: Trouble and loss. Seen near handle: unfaithfulness.

Owl

Oyster: Long engagement.

Pail: Hard marriage but loving.

Palm tree: Happy and contented life, respect.

Palm tree

Pear: Comfort.

Pig: Good and bad luck together.

Pipe: Long life and happiness.

Pump: Generous nature.

Purse: Money.

Question Mark: Hesitancy.

Rake: Tidy up affairs and methods.

Rat: Treachery, loss, clever enemies.

Rattle: Many children.

Ring

Raven: Trouble through gossip.

Ring: If near top: wedding. If near middle: marriage ahead. If at bottom: long engagement.

Rose: Lucky life and love.

Saw: Hard work.

Scales

Saucer: Contented married life.

Scales: Involvement with the law. If seen unbalanced: injustice.

Scepter: Authority.

Scissors: Quarrels, separation.

Spider

Scythe: Danger.

Ship: Travel.

Snake: Trouble and misfortune, hatred.

Spade: Wealth through steady work.

Spider: Unexpected money, determination.

Spoon

Spoon: Christening.

Square: Restriction.

Star: Joy, prosperity. One with five points: success without joy. One with eight points: bad omen.

Star

Sun: Health, wealth, and happiness.

Swan: A lover, contented life.

Sword: Arguments at home and in business.

Table: Party, social gathering. If dots nearby: business meeting.

Teapot: Discussions.

Telescope: Plan for the future.

Tent: Time to rest.

Thistle: Happy without riches.

Toad: Drop negative people and flatterers.

Tortoise: Difficulties, but will be overcome.

Tree: Good health; plans will be successful.

Triangle: Pointed upward: success. Pointed downward: plans go wrong.

Trident: Success with maritime matters.

Trunk: Happiness at the end of a journey.

Umbrella: Open: good luck through friendships. Closed: friendship denied.

Vase: Good deeds bring future reward.

Violets: Love.

Violin: Individualism, egoism.

Wall: Lover's quarrel.

Watch: Secret admirer.

Wheel: Promotion.

Windmill: Enterprise and work will bring success.

Wings: Message, news.

Wolf: Greed.

Woman: Happy family; many: gossip, scandal.

Sword

Triangle

Violin

Runes

Runes are enjoying a well-deserved renaissance among New Age followers, Witches, and those practicing the magickal arts. A principal reason for the sudden popularity of Runes is due to their accessibility. Anyone can make a set of runes, and just as quickly learn to use them.

The word *rune* derives from the Old Norse *run* which means "secret." The Runes were an ancient Germanic alphabet, once used for normal writing, as well as mystical and divination purposes. The Vikings used Runes to protect their homes, as well as add power to their swords and shields. The Shamans of Scandinavia used them in healing, to cast spells, and to protect burial mounds.

The Runes consist of twenty-four letters together with one blank Rune. The twenty-four Runes are dedicated to three Norse deities and are divided into sets of eight known as Freyr's Aett,[2] Hagal's Aett, and Tyr's Aett. The twenty-fifth, or blank Rune, is called Wyrd and symbolizes the unknowable, or destiny. The traditional meaning of the Wyrd Rune is, "in the lap of the Gods," or "What will be, will be."

Professionally crafted Rune sets can be purchased at almost any New Age or occult book store. These are nice because they come with an instruction book and storage pouch. However, it is just as easy to make your own and infuse them with your energy in the process.

Flat, evenly shaped stones, ceramic tiles, wooden sticks, or self-hardening clay all make wonderful sets of Runes. Once they are painted or engraved with the appropriate Rune symbol, they become just as magickal as any store-bought item. If you choose to make a set of Runes, you will also need to make a cloth pouch to keep them in. Choose a heavy fabric, such as velvet or leather, which will both protect and energize your Runes when not in use.

---

[2] Aett: family or genus, used as both a name for the threefold divisions of the futhark and the eight divisions of the heavens. Also means "group" or "divisions of eight."

Rune Stone Meanings

Freyr's Aett (First Eight Runes)

1. Wunjo: Joy.

   Joy and happiness coming into your life. Success. Good news. Joy in one's work. Affection from a loved one.
   Reversed: Opposite of the above.

2. Gebo: Partnership.

   There could be a gift involved. Always a positive sign because there is no reverse involved. Important development in a romantic relationship. Could mean a marriage or business partnership.
   Reversed: There is no reverse. Same as above.

3. Kano: Open.

   Friendly and warm. Strength, energy, and power. Positive action. Problems and troubles solved easily. Good things coming into your life. Good time to start something new.
   Reversed: Opposite of the above.

4. Raido: Journey.

   The original meaning was "wagon," which meant travel. Travel with pleasure, without problems. Possible journey of the soul. Period of logical thought. A good time to buy or sell.
   Reversed: Opposite of the above.

5. Ansuz: Signals.

   The spoken word or heading advice. The original meaning was "mouth." A time to think before speaking. Eloquence and ease. Discovery of secret ability.
   Reversed: Lies, trickery, general deceit. Get a second opinion.

6. Thurisaz: Gateway.

Unexpected good luck. Good health. Protection. Warns against headstrong action.

Reversed: No desire to heed the warnings about headstrong action; will press on regardless. Your luck is running out. Self-deception.

7. Uruz: Strength.

Original meaning, "wild ox." Virility, good health, and strong resistance. Of strong emotions. Could be recovering from ill health. Not much improvement in business matters. Could be a promotion.

Reversed: Imminent failure. Weak will. Low vitality. Could be a small illness.

8. Fehu: Possessions.

The original meaning was "cattle," which were the measure of an individual's worth and standing. Signifies material gain, could mean wealth. Goals are now within your grasp. Ability to overcome opposition.

Reversed: Loss or disappointment. Frustration.

Hagal's Aett (Second Eight Runes)

9. Sowelu: Wholeness.

Progress and success. Possible travel. Success with examinations. Good health. Recovery from illness. Conquest, victory, and power.

Reversed: Warning against overworking. Be more considerate of your loved ones.

10. Algiz: Protection.

Unexpected help from an unsympathetic person when it is most needed. A time to stand your ground. Be careful to hold tight to your principles. Invincibility.

Reversed: Vulnerability. Possible loss or injustice.

11. Perth: Initiation.

Secrets. Psychic powers. An unforeseen turn of events. Possible news from afar. A joyful reunion with someone from the past.
Reversed: Disappointment.

12. Eithwaz: Defense.

Try to look ahead, anticipate what is coming. A time of difficulty which will require tact and diplomacy. After a slight delay, things will improve.
Reversed: Warning, be ever watchful.

13. Jera: Harvest.

You will reap the benefits of your efforts. A time to receive what has been well earned. A good time to finalize a contract or complete a task. Financial matters will improve in the days to come.
Reversed: Slight delay in financial improvement, could be a slight disappointment.

14. Isa: Standstill.

The "ice" Rune. Like ice, this Rune indicates that you should remain still. You may be on thin ice, so it is best not to move. A time of patience and understanding. Temporary parting. Sacrifice. Submission.
Reversed: The ice is beginning to thaw; things will improve.

15. Naurthiz: Constraint.

A bad time to embark on any new venture. Avoid anything which seems to be a bargain or a quick way of making money without effort. Now is the time for patience and planning.
Reversed: A time for caution. Think before acting. Make no moves at this time. If you have made an unwise choice, cut your losses and call it a day.

16. Hagalaz: Disruption.
                  Unforeseen forces are working against you; be
                  careful. Be prepared for an unpleasant surprise.
                  Use caution.
                  Reversed: You will be able to ride this one out.
                  Keep fighting and don't lose focus.

Tyr's Aett (Third Eight Runes)

17. Othila: Separation.
                  Separation in the sense of moving in a new
                  direction at this time. There could be an inher-
                  itance, or a business deal on the horizon. The
                  future is changing.
                  Reversed: There could be financial disputes or
                  opposition to a plan.

18. Dagaz: Breakthrough.
                  A time of transformation. Freedom. A weight has
                  been lifted from your shoulders. You will win,
                  even when the odds are stacked against you.
                  Positive changes are coming.
                  Reversed: At last you can see the light at the end
                  of the tunnel. Changes may be slow but are still
                  coming.

19. Inguz: Fertility.
                  A goal realized. A problem solved. Time to rel-
                  ish in the victory of a job well done. Take a rest
                  and reflect.
                  Reversed: There is no reverse. Same as above.

20. Laguz: Flow.
                  A long journey may be in the offing. A trip
                  overseas. Time to go with the flow, and instincts.
                  Feel rather than think.
                  Reversed: Heed good advice from others. Look
                  out for temptation. Not a good sign.

21. Mannaz: Self.

Time to think about yourself. Plan changes. A good time to change employment or residence. You are making steady progress.

Reversed: Keep your emotions in control at this time, changes may be postponed.

22. Ehwaz: Movement.

New beginnings. A time of excitement. Change is in the air. Travel. A good time to keep things in perspective. You feel confident.

Reversed: Be mindful of others and keep emotions in check.

23. Berkana: Growth.

New energies are present. New ventures are on the horizon. Could mean birth or pregnancy for a woman. New and fresh ideas. Possible sign of marriage. A favorable time.

Reversed: Keep a keen eye out for family problems. Disruptions with friends, anxiety, or relationships.

24. Teiwaz: Warrior.

A time to move forward and experience an adventure. New things on the horizon. A time to be bold and courageous. Victory can be yours. A time of great passion.

Reversed: There could be a loss in business. Stagnation. A time of raw emotions, take care and be careful.

25. Wyrd: The Last Rune—The Blank Rune.

The Unknowable. Fate. This Rune tells you to place your fate with the gods. There is nothing you can do at this time. Fate is power. You must let be what will be. Your problem or situation is way beyond your control at this time. "In the lap of the gods" signifies powerful changes, changes

which are out of your control. There is no
reverse for this Rune. Use the other Runes in
your reading for advice.

Rune Layout Patterns

One-Rune Method: This is by far the easiest method for reading
the Runes, especially if you have a specific question which needs
immediate attention. Cup the Runes in your hand, concentrate on
your question, and then ask it aloud. Place the Runes back in their
pouch and mix them thoroughly. Dip into the pouch and pull out
one Rune only. This will be the answer to your question.

The nice thing about the Runes, and this particular method,
is that you can use them anywhere. So if you are at work and
having a problem with someone or something, use your break
time to consult the Runes. They will provide you with a quick
solution to set things right again.

Three-Rune Method: This method is very much like the first.
Cup the Runes in your hand, concentrate on your question, and
then ask it aloud. Place the Runes
back in the pouch and mix them
thoroughly. Pull three Runes from
the pouch and place them in front
of you (see diagram). The first
Rune, to the left, indicates the
basis of the problem, or present
situation. The middle Rune shows
the vibrations currently surrounding you. The last Rune, the one
you placed to the right, gives you the answer, or may suggest the
proper action to be taken.

Three-Rune Method Layout

The Runic Cross Method: Cup the Runes in your hand, concentrate on your question, and then speak it aloud. Put the Runes
back in the pouch and mix them thoroughly. Pull five Runes from
the pouch, one at a time. Lay the first three out in a row from left
to right. The fourth goes above the center stone, and the fifth is
placed below the center stone. All five stones should be face down.

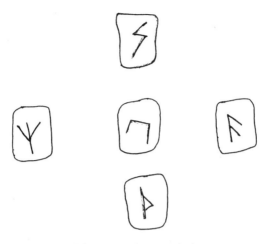

The Runic Cross Method

Turn the center stone up; this represents the present situation and what is going on now. The stone to the left is the past. Turn this stone over next; it will tell you what past vibrations are still affecting the present situation.

The top stone is next. This stone explains what outside help, or self-help, is necessary to improve the situation as it stands. Now turn over the bottom stone. This stone will tell you what changes can or cannot be expected.

The last stone to be turned over is the one on the right arm of the cross. This stone represents the future—the final outcome of the reading. For more clarification, pull a sixth Rune. This Rune is placed at the bottom of the cross, under the fifth stone. This sixth Rune will denote new, fresh influences that could affect the situation and its final outcome.

Thoughts and Ideas

The ability to accurately predict the future is what gives the Witch his or her edge. Divination is one of the keys to basic occult knowledge, and has always been considered an important part of magickal training. By learning to divine the future, the Witch is able to weigh the ramifications of his or her intentions before they are put into action.

Think about all the times you have said "if I had only known." Think of all the distress you could have avoided "if you had only known" the right thing to say, or the right move to make, in advance. This is why divination is such an important part of Witchcraft. It is the only way you can see for yourself, beforehand, what is going to happen. Divination gives you the ability to make informed decisions which, in turn, will help you avoid costly mistakes.

If you are new to Witchcraft, and uncertain about which method of divination to choose, start with the Runes. They are easy to make, convenient to use, and there is very little left up to personal interpretation. Because of their size, they travel well. They can be read almost anywhere, and in any situation. Keep a set of Runes in your purse, briefcase, or school locker. Use your coffee break, lunch hour, or recess time to consult them about the events of the day.

The best way to become proficient with the Runes, or any of the divination systems mentioned, is by using them on a regular basis. Before you leave for work or start your day, take a moment to consult your Runes, cards, or tea leaves. You don't need to be in a crisis to seek higher wisdom or spiritual guidance. Use your divination skills to help set daily and weekly goals, or to indicate areas where personal progress can be made. A simple question like "What should I work on today?" will provide you with the motivation and direction needed to live the magickal life.

Part III

The Secrets of
Modern Witchcraft

11

The Color of Magick

The purest and most thoughtful minds are those which love color.

—John Ruskin (1819–1900), English art critic and author

Color exerts a powerful influence on our minds and emotions. It is an integral part of self-expression and creativity. Color inspires our thoughts, excites our emotions, and calms our fears. Almost everything we do, every sensation we feel, is in some way affected by color. Color plays an important part in all our lives. It is therefore essential to understand it.

All colors have a certain energy frequency at which they vibrate. It is this vibration that produces an effect. Because color is an important part of life, it can be incorporated into magickal spells and rituals.

The Color of Magick

Red is primarily a color of energy and expansion. It is the color of sexual expression. On a positive level it creates life and gives us energy. In its negative aspect it represents anger, war, and destruction. Red is associated with the survival instinct, the sensation of sensual pleasure and lust.

Pink is a mixture of red and white, or white reflecting the subtle side of red. Pink softens the sexual and survival desire. It provides a feeling of loving protection. Pink is friendly love rather than lust. It helps express the desire to share one's feelings with another. On a positive level, pink emanates true love and compassion. Relationships built on pink vibrations are far superior to those built mainly on red, or sexual, energy.

Orange is a combination of red and yellow; red being the physical energy and yellow its mental partner. Orange is assertive and projects rational potential. When in a negative state, it can be too rigid in its ideals and direction. Orange is associated with the ability to reason, as it contemplates how to logically survive.

Gold is the higher octave of orange. Gold is the light of joy and cheer. Hope, laughter, and happiness emanate from gold. Gold serves to communicate love and truth to others. When inspired, gold can be a great artist, as it radiates warmth and love to the world. Gold is considered perfection and the wisdom of the ages.

Yellow is the color of analytical energy, knowledge, logic, and the ability to learn. Yellow, like the sun, awakens and stimulates mental activity. Everyone needs yellow to encourage rational thinking. Yellow is attraction and desire. Too much yellow can cause you to be dictatorial on the mental plane. Too little yellow, and you revert to instinct rather than logic. Yellow is associated with the ability to receive and broadcast individual telepathic response. Yellow desires to learn, know, and teach.

Green, the color of nature, signifies self-healing and the process of regeneration. Green is restful. It allows you time to replenish your energy reserves. Green is related to the feminine principle, and teaches love. Green is associated with your ability to appreciate and receive love. Too much green causes conceit, and lack of consideration for others. Green is the bridge between the physical, survival-oriented body, and the mental, spiritually-oriented body.

Brown is the color of the soil. It represents the energy reserves of nature and the desire for regeneration, as all life begins in the green state, then matures, and eventually turns brown in the effort to be reabsorbed. Brown helps to stabilize your material wealth. It balances out what should be shared, or given back to the earth, or to the society from where it came. Brown approached from the negative standpoint leads to greed and the restriction of material progress.

Blue, the color of the sky, is the color of mystery and wonderment. It awakens the emotions to the spiritual side of nature. Blue is the desire to seek the unknown and your spiritual nature. Too much blue can cause you to become absentminded, disoriented, and unable to relate to reality. Blue is good for important decision-making situations, as well as for ethical reflection.

Violet, or purple, is the color of royalty, spiritual growth, and philosophy. The crown of our intelligence and where we get our spiritual ideals from is considered to be violet. Violet on a negative plane creates chaos and secretive actions. Violet is the energy of red coupled with the wisdom and thinking ability of blue. Violet allows us to transcend the mundane and enter the spiritual realms. Violet is spiritual reflection and devotional piety.

Black, the absence of color, is the opposite of white, which reflects all colors. Black absorbs color. Black is the color of secrets and the unknown. This is why black is considered to be sexy. Black creates a mystery all its own; it is the color that hides things. Too much black will make you withdrawn and listless. It has a tendency to absorb your energy, as it detaches you from the world of color.

White, the carrier for the other colors, is the combination of all the colors of the spectrum. White is purity, innocence, that which lies barren awaiting the seed of life. White is the color of creation. White reflects your inner qualities and true nature.

Warm and Cool Colors

Color is usually referred to as either warm and active, or cool and passive. Warm colors give off energy, they stimulate everything within their range. Warm colors tend to make you feel strong, active, and energetic. Cool colors, on the other hand, seem to be more intellectual, inspirational, and spiritual.

The warm colors are red, pink, yellow and orange. The cool colors are blue, purple, violet, and brown. Green is in the middle, as it can either be cool, when it runs to the blue side, or warm, when it is mixed with yellow.

White is considered warm, while black is considered cool. White and black represent the positive and active, and negative and passive, sides of life and nature.

Working with Color

Clothing is an important part of everyone's life. It makes a statement about your personal taste, lifestyle, and status. Clothing keeps you warm in the winter, accentuates the body, and camouflages undesirable qualities. Your clothes speak to those you meet even before you are able to.

Color, design, and texture all play a part in the clothing you wear and the image you try to convey. Nicely tailored suits, in earth-tone colors, give the impression of conservative and traditional deportment. Flashy colors in bold patterns tend to give the impression of extravagant and outrageous behavior. Dirty, untidy, and disheveled clothing tells people you are sloppy, careless, and indolent. It may not be politically correct to judge others by the way they dress, but everyone ultimately judges others by their appearance.

Areas of the Body

When analyzing your wardrobe, it is important to understand the different areas which need clothing. Each part of the body conveys a different message to those around you, and so will the clothing you choose to cover that area. The five areas of the body are:

- The upper inner body
- The upper outer body
- The lower inner body
- The lower outer body
- The head and feet

The upper body is the portion of the body above the waistline. This includes the arms, hands, and head. The upper body represents the conscious way in which you express yourself and how you relate to others. This is the area which gives you the most control over your environment. This is where your center of command resides, which is intrinsically your ability to reason and choose.

The upper inner body clothing (underwear) reflects the emotional situation or environment you wish existed, or would like to create. This clothing also makes a statement as to your emotional well-being and sense of self.

The upper outer body clothing (blouses, shirts, vests, sweaters, and coats) reflects the emotional conditions and situations you feel most comfortable with. Outer garments which hang from the upper body, such as coats, jackets, and sweaters, protect you from inclement weather and give you a sense of security.

The lower body is a reflection of your physical state and represents your material and physical needs. The movement from the waist down involves not only the regenerative sexual organs, but also the legs and feet, which carry you from one environment to another.

The inner lower body clothing (underwear) is how you wish you could relate to your physical surroundings. This area also expresses your sexual fears and desires.

The outer lower body clothing (slacks and skirts) shows how you react to your surroundings, and what you would like others to think about you. The clothing on this area symbolically protects the ego, just as the physical clothing shields the body from adverse conditions.

It is important to note that the upper and lower bodies communicate their needs to each other. When in need, one will take over for the other. This is an important point to remember when combining colors. It is always good to keep a balance between the upper, emotional body, and the lower, physical body.

Color Dressing Hints

- *Footwear:* Conscious recognition of areas that you need to control.
  Wear brown for control, red for show and sexual desire, blue for emotional stability, and black to hide vulnerabilities.

- *Leg wear, Including Socks and Stockings:* This is the subconscious recognition of areas you wish you were in control of, something to strive toward.
  Wear red for sexual desire and attention; pink for friendship and warmth; yellow when seeking self-assurance; green for tranquility; blue for emotional stability; brown for a sense of well-being; and black to create an air of mystery.

- *Pants and Skirts:* The conscious direction in which you are moving, where the physical self is going, and where it wants to go. Wear white for admiration from others; red for physical attraction and sexual excitement; pink to express feelings of love and friendship; orange for more control; yellow to reflect logic and clear thinking; green to demonstrate strength and the willingness to help others; blue for stability and to reflect personal emotional control; brown to reflect a sense of security and stability; black for mystery and sexual attraction.

- *Shirts, Blouses, and Vests:* These are the subconscious emotional energies you live and deal with. Some of these you are able to control, others you try to.

Wear white to express truth and your sense of honesty; red for sexual and sensual attention and attraction; pink for attracting friends and to express contentment; yellow to signify logical thinking and to attract others to your point of view; green for healing and to conserve energy; blue for emotional support and to hide shyness; brown for control and stability; black for mystery and sexual attraction; violet or purple to express mental power.

- *Coats, Jackets, and Sweaters:* These are your conscious, emotional feelings. Emotions you are able to express and share with others. Wear white for attraction and the expression of honesty; red for attraction, strength, and personal power; pink to aid with friendships; blue for peace and security; green to contain and reserve energy; brown to stabilize and maintain balance; black to absorb energy and project an air of mystery; violet or purple for personal power.

- *Underwear:* These are your private, personal, sexual expressions of the inner self, which remains protected by the ego, as well as the clothing which covers it. Wear white for protection and the expression of honesty; red for sexual attraction; pink to develop long and lasting friendships; yellow to communicate your ideas and get your point across; green to reserve energy and maintain health; blue for emotional control and a sense of security; black to excite and stimulate sexual activity; violet or purple to gain power over others.

The Personality of Color

Color plays an important role in all our lives. It is an integral part of our self-expression and a reflection of our inner selves. The colors we wear and choose to surround ourselves with are a visible reflection of our true personality.

The appropriate use of color in magick can greatly enhance the effectiveness of just about any spell or rite. Try to plan your rituals and magickal works around a color theme. Coordinate your clothing, candle, and altar colors so that everything projects the same vibration. This will help you create pure and powerful thought-forms for your magickal intentions.

Make colors part of your life. Use the following chart to find out which colors are predominant in your life. By breaking your name down into single digits, as in numerology, and then attributing a color to each digit, your own personal rainbow emerges. By adding all of the corresponding numbers together you will then get one single number. This is your personal number, and the equivalent of your dominant color.

PERSONALITY COLOR AND NUMBER CHART

Letters	Numbers	Colors
A J S	1	Red
B K T	2	Orange
C L U	3	Yellow
D M V	4	Green
E N W	5	Blue
F O X	6	Indigo
G P Y	7	Violet
H Q Z	8	Pink
I R	9	Gold

Example: Sabrina

Name:	S	A	B	R	I	N	A
Number:	1	1	2	9	9	5	1
Color:	Red	Red	Orange	Gold	Gold	Blue	Red

Total Number: 28—broken down to a single digit is:
   2+8=10, 1+0 = 1.

The predominant number is one, and the color for the name Sabrina is red. The secondary color of importance is gold. It helps to soften the overwhelming power of the red vibration.

The Color of Personal Expression

Red: Creative, pioneer, leader.

Red needs to be its own master, stand on its own two feet, and express its creativity. Red is ambition. If red is forced to follow, it will become frustrated and angry. Red will always live life to the fullest because of its depth of passion and aggressive nature.

Orange: Peacemaker, organizer, cooperative.

Orange has the energy and interest to delve into situations, dissect the components, and then organize the situation. Orange is tactful and has a talent for persuasion. Orange has a sense of the esthetic and longs for peace. Orange likes balance and can be very demanding because it has a tendency to be sensitive.

Yellow: Intellectual, dreamer, creative.

Yellow is a dreamer. Yellow builds castles in the sky and tends to flights of fancy. Yellow likes to press forward; the future is yellow's reality. Yellow likes to express itself in an intellectual way. Yellow is refined and very charming. Yellow likes to be popular and usually has a wide circle of friends.

Green: Nature-loving, tranquil, understanding.

Green understands that life has a purpose and creates a purpose for its own well-being. Green is very patient, understanding, and pays attention to detail. Green is a down-to-earth person who likes to create and achieve results. Green has the tendency to get caught up in its own ideas and become dogmatic. Green likes to take the time to nourish and reflect.

Blue: Spiritual, dependable, a free spirit.

Blue believes in truth and objective reality. Blue builds its life on devotion and its connection with the universal environment. Blue seeks the truth in everything it touches. Blue takes an active interest in the world and becomes involved with understanding life. Blue seeks to know, learn, and experience. Blue needs to be aware, indulging its own whims.

Indigo: Spiritual leader, philosopher, lover.

Indigo senses the beauty in all things. Indigo must express beauty, love, and understanding to others. Love is very important to indigo, because without love it feels there is no purpose to life. Indigo understands life and how to solve its problems with little effort. Indigo can easily get off track by removing itself from the turbulence of life and refusing to assume personal responsibility.

Violet: Spiritual perception and the inspired mind.

Violet must know the reason why. It searches the hidden and occult side of life. Violet is sensitive to others' vibrations and is always in search of a tranquil environment. Violet is the light-bearer and brings the gift of the spirit to mankind. Violet must be careful not to drift off and just live in its dreams. Violet is very personal and does not mix well in a crowd. Violet tends to live in a fantasy world, and though it can be charming and delightful, it seldom finds reason to be so.

Pink: Friend, lover, administrator.

Pink is everyone's friend. Pink is able to blend the spiritual and material sides of nature effortlessly. Pink harbors few illusions and always understands what it must to maintain. Pink is able to judge, and arbitrate between factions. Pink is also able to blend physical drive with spiritual need. Pink needs to achieve and will stop at nothing to get what it thinks it needs. Pink will also help others achieve their dreams. Pink likes to achieve.

Gold: Intellect, energy, cosmic love.

Gold is the hope of the world. Gold is happiness and joy. Gold seems to spread good cheer wherever it goes. Gold must share its beauty, love of life, and general good nature with everyone it comes in contact with. Gold is also the master teacher. Gold is popular, well liked, and always above petty desires. Gold does have a problem with living up to others' ideals and sense of perfection. Gold will become disappointed when it thinks it has failed to impress.

Color and Candle Magic

The history of candle burning is as old as humanity itself and originates from fire worship. Early man was in awe of fire; it warmed him, protected him, and helped him cook his food.

The flame of the hearth was carefully guarded, shielded against the ravages of wind and rain. Fire came to represent strength, power, and the ability to see past the terrors of night.

The flame of a candle is automatically magickal, as it brings light to darkness. Symbolically, candles are illumination, as they represent the vitalizing power of the sun and the spark of life within the individual soul. Just as the flame consumes the wax, so candles illustrate the relationship between spirit and matter.

Candles can be used by themselves as a form of magick, or they may be incorporated as part of a spell. In either case, the candle itself becomes the point of focus. The color of the candle, its shape and size, all play an important role in the art of candle magick. The color signifies the intent, its design or shape represents the objective, and its size is equivalent to the amount of time needed for burning.

Color is of primary importance in candle magick. There are twelve basic colors which offer different sensory vibrations, red being the most physically potent and powerful, violet the most passive and spiritually receptive. The primary colors of the light spectrum (red, orange, yellow, green, blue, indigo, and violet) emit specific energies which are symbolic of their intrinsic value. These colors move energy outward and forward, as well as inward and backward.

In addition to the seven primary colors, there are five additional colors used in the art of candle magick. These are black, white, gray, pink, and brown. Black anchors and absorbs; white encourages and supports; gray is seldom used because it is considered to be void, without movement; pink attracts and entices; brown stabilizes and sustains.

Burning time (how long a candle should burn) is as essential to candle magick as color is. Each color of the spectrum has its own special wavelength or vibrational frequency. This vibrational frequency is the equivalent of motion and energy, which is the amount of time needed to activate a spell. Therefore, a candle which requires a burning time of four hours will take four times longer to work than a candle which requires only one hour to

burn. However, the longer it takes a spell to work, and the more
energy involved in its formulation, the more enduring are its results.

The following chart explains the color significance and burning times for candles.

CANDLE COLOR CHART

Candle Color	Meaning of the Color	Necessary Burning Time
Red	Courage, strength, survival, power, lust, immediate action	One hour
Pink	Love, friendship, an open heart, calm emotions	One hour
Orange	Action, attraction, selling, bringing about desired results	Two hours
Yellow	Communication, selling oneself, persuasion, attraction	Three hours
Green	Love, fertility, money, luck, health, personal goals	Four hours
Blue	Creativity, tranquility, peace, perception	Three hours
Indigo	Wisdom, self-awareness, psychic abilities	Two hours
Violet	Power, ambition, tension, spiritual development	One hour
Black	Protection, the return or release of negativity, power	One hour
Brown	Stability, grounding, earth rites, to create indecision	Four hours
White	The universal color, can be used for any work, all general candle magick	No set time
Gold	Prosperity, attraction, wealth, increase	One hour

In addition to their differences in color, candles also come in
a variety of shapes other than the simple household taper. There
are image candles in the shape of men and women, animal shapes,

such as the cat, candles which have been notched or made into knobs, and even candles that are shaped like skulls. It is a good idea to use the symbolic candles whenever possible. Because they are already formed into an image of your desire, they make the visualization process of your spell all that much easier.

Symbolic Image Candle Chart

Candle Shape	Symbolic Purpose
Cat	To change one's luck. Black cat—change of luck from bad to good; green cat—good luck with money and gambling; red cat—good luck with love interest.
Crucifix or Cross	Used as altar candles and for last rites
Devil (image of)	To exorcize evil, release negative holds
Double Action	To attract favorable circumstances and repel negative influences at the same time
Human Image	Used to represent the individual the spell is being worked on. Red for love and passion; pink for friendships to acquire; green for healing and marriage; black for releasing or stopping negative actions; white for blessing and spiritual union.
Red Witch	Burned in matters of love, or to reverse the negative actions of others.
Seven Knob	One knob burned each day to make a wish come true. Red knob—lust, passion, power; green knob—love, money, health; black knob—protection, reversing, and separation.
Skull	Spiritual enlightenment, healing, channeling
The Seven Day	Glass-encased novena. Used for the specific purpose printed on the candle glass. Burned for seven days to ensure the petitioner his or her wish.

Color burning times are applicable to symbolic candles.

Working With Candles

The first step in candle magick is to choose a candle by selecting a color and shape which represents your desire. Next you will have to dress the candle. This is done by anointing the entire candle with a special oil. The oil is usually made of some plant or flower which also represents your desire (see the next chapter for recipes). Place some of the oil on your fingertips. As you concentrate on your desire, rub the oil onto the candle, starting from the center and rubbing upward. Then rub the oil from the center downward. Be sure to cover the entire candle with the oil as you infuse it with your desire.

When you are planning a candle-magick spell, try to keep all of your symbolism or vibrations the same. For example, if you are doing a love spell, you would want to use a red image candle and love-drawing oil. If you were trying to open up the lines of communication between you and another person, you might want to try a yellow candle and mercury oil. For a peaceful home, use a blue candle and tranquility oil. The whole idea is to keep your colors, objects, and thoughts similar in meaning and symbolism. By doing this, your energy is focused for maximum effect.

Candle Magick Hints

- Whenever possible, make your own candles. While the wax is in a liquid form, add a corresponding oil, herb, or flower. For example, if you are doing a money spell you could add heliotrope oil and mint leaves.

- When dressing the candle, close your eyes and concentrate. Visualize, see in your mind's eye what the candle represents.

- Always keep in mind, and allow for, the burning time of the candle.

Candle Spells

Be sure to read through the spell you will be doing several times. Don't forget to make your ritual checklist, and organize all items needed prior to the work. Last, but not least, you are the best judge of what you need and are able to maintain. If you doubt what you are doing or feel bad about it, then you have no business doing it. On the other hand, if it feels right and you are willing to accept responsibility for your actions, then *go for it!*

The Love Box

Items needed: a small heart-shaped box, love-drawing incense and censer, love-drawing oil, a large pink candle and holder, parchment paper, pen, rose quartz, some of your own hair, orris root powder, charcoal, and matches.

Perform this spell on the first Friday after the moon turns new. Begin by taking your ritual bath. Before doing the spell, meditate and visualize the type of lover you wish to attract. Light the charcoal, place some of the incense on it, and again visualize the type of individual you wish to attract. Inscribe on the parchment that which you desire in a lover. Place some more incense on the coals. Now dress the pink candle with the love-drawing oil as you chant the following:

> *May the Gods of love hear my plea*
> *And bring everlasting love to me!*

Light the candle and read your petition aloud, then place the candle on top of the parchment paper. Place more incense on the coals. Meditate on your wish, and when finished, read the following:

> *Hail to thee, goddess of love,*
> *Shine down on me from above.*
> *Bring now a lover to me,*
> *As I will, so it shall be.*

Let all items remain until the candle has burned out. Fill the heart-shaped box with the following items: one pinch of incense, seven drops of oil, the parchment paper, rose quartz, some candle drippings, your hair, and some of the orris root powder. The box is now left where it will be most effective. (An office worker could place the box in her desk. Or, just leave the box on your nightstand, next to the bed.)

Candle Love Spell

Items needed: a picture of the desired one, and some of their hair and handwriting to use as relics. You will also need a red cloth pouch, one red image candle (sexually aligned to the gender you wish to attract), rose petals, and rose oil.

Place the candle in front of you with the picture and all of the needed items in front of it. Dress the candle with the rose oil as you visualize your lover coming closer to you and being more attentive. When you feel the time is right, light the candle and chant the following to build power and energy. Direct this energy into the candle:

Candle of power,
From this hour,
Bring unto me
The love that I see.
That he (she) shall requite
My attentions this night,
Let him (her) see only me.
As I will, so mote it be!

Allow the candle to burn completely out. Carry the pouch filled with the rose petals and your lover's items with you whenever you are going to be together. It is also a good idea to wear some of the rose oil.

Spell to Attract Money

Items needed: a green candle,[1] five silver coins, a small jar filled with sea water, your magick wand, and some matches.

---

[1]Green candle: it is best to use small, fast-burning decorative tapers. These can be purchased at Hallmark gift shops, New Age book stores, and occult outlets.

On the night of the full moon, go into a wooded area, to a spot where four paths cross. Here you will inscribe with your wand a large circle with a pentagram in the center. Dig a small hole in the very center and place the jar in it so the top half is exposed to the moonlight. Place the green candle on top of the jar. Light it as you chant the following:

> *My Lady of the Abundant Sea,*
> *Bring me wealth and prosperity.*

Now take the silver coins and place one on each point of the pentagram as you chant the following:

> *Silver coins that sparkle bright,*
> *Increase my wealth from this night.*

When the candle is completely burned out, open the jar. Pick up each of the silver coins, one at a time, and place them into the jar as you chant the following:

> *Earth to sea, Earth to sea,*
> *Bring me the money I see.*
> *As I will, so mote it be.*

Sprinkle several drops of water on the ground as you thank the Goddess for her blessings. Bring the water home with you and anoint yourself with it every day until it is gone.

Spirit-Guide Channeling

This simple spell will enable you to contact your spirit guide or help to get messages or information from the cosmos.

Items needed: one white skull candle, angelic vibrations incense, spirit oil, a pillow or meditation mat, a dish or incense burner filled with white sand, and a charcoal.

Arrange a special space for the skull candle. It should be either on a shelf or a pedestal, high enough so that when you are sitting on your meditation mat or pillow, you have to look up to see the candle. Place the dish for incense between the mat and the candle.

Be sure that you will not be disturbed. Turn down the lights. Stand behind the mat (or pillow) and take several deep, relaxing breaths to get yourself into the mood to contact higher forces.

Take the candle and dress it with the spirit oil, charging life into the candle. Make the candle a receptacle for the spirit (or universal consciousness) which will soon inhabit it. Then place it on the shelf or pedestal. Take several deep breaths and feel the atmosphere in the room change to become a chamber of spirituality. Now light the candle and say the following:

> *O Lord of Life, Goddess of Delight*
> *Open my mind, let my soul take flight*
> *That now your knowledge shall come through*
> *As my thoughts and essence become one with you.*
> *So shall it be!*

Sit down on the mat or pillow. Take several more deep breaths and relax. Place some incense on the charcoal and begin to merge with the candle. Visualize the energy of the cosmos forming a swirling cone of white light above the skull. See this energy funnel down into the skull, giving it life and a personality of its own. Then draw this energy from the skull in a stream of light, making a connection between you and the skull. It is through this connection that the information you are seeking will travel. Relax and allow yourself to accept the information which is being transmitted. Record all information which has been received by keeping a journal. When all has been completed, snuff out the candle and put all the items away.

Peaceful-Home Spell

This spell is especially useful for those who entertain for business. There are times when people of varying viewpoints may need to come together in a social atmosphere. To keep things running smoothly, harmoniously, and peacefully, use this spell prior to the gathering.

Items needed: one blue candle, tranquility oil, and sandalwood incense.

One hour before the occasion, take your ritual bath. As you are doing this, visualize the guests as they arrive. See in your mind's eye the evening progressing and everyone having a wonderful time. When your bath is completed, anoint your solar plexus with the tranquility oil. This will help you project positive and harmonious energy throughout the evening.

Take the blue candle and place it in the room where most of the evening's activities will be held. Now take the incense, light it, and carry it throughout the house or apartment. Move from room to room, saying:

> *Queen of Heaven, Star of the Sea,*
> *Fill this house with love and harmony.*
> *Silver Goddess enthroned above*
> *Let all gather here in peace and love.*
> *So Shall It Be!*

Now enter the room where you have placed the blue candle and light it. Walk around that room four times in a deosil (clockwise) fashion chanting, just as you did in the other rooms. Place the incense next to the candle and wait for your guests.

Black Cat Fast-Luck Spell

This spell is easy to do and can work wonders if you are having a period of bad luck.

Items needed: one black cat candle, black cat oil, and a mirror.

On the night of the waxing moon, as close to midnight as possible, begin the spell. On your altar or other flat surface, place the mirror reflecting side up. Dress the black cat candle with the black cat oil. As you do this, visualize your luck changing and good things coming to you. Next, place the cat candle on the mirror and light it as you chant the following:

> *Black cat power*
> *From this hour*
> *Reflect the light.*
> *Make things right.*

Allow the black cat candle to burn for one hour. Repeat this spell every night, at the same time, until the full moon. On the night of the full moon, place the mirror with the black cat on it in the moonlight. Repeat the chant and allow the candle to burn out. When the candle has been consumed, discard any wax left and put the mirror away.

Thoughts and Ideas

Candle and color magick can be practiced anywhere and anytime. They require a minimum amount of preparation and skill. Even under the most rigid living conditions, candle magick can escape notice. Remember, being a Witch is about being clever and creative. If you are in a situation in which it is impossible to practice your craft openly, then you must use your imagination. For example, for the Peaceful-Home Spell, use a blue air freshener candle. They can be purchased at your local grocery store and are very attractive.

If your spell calls for a yellow candle, which must burn for three hours, plan your magick to coincide with outdoor activities. Use a yellow mosquito-repelling candle. Dress the top of the candle with your oil and then inscribe your desire into the soft wax near the wick. Light the candle and place it on the porch or patio. For that late-night rendezvous with a loved one, use pink tapers on the table. They only need to burn for one hour, just about the time it takes to enjoy an intimate meal.

Take advantage of the fireplace. Write out your wish on a small piece of parchment paper, place a few drops of oil on it, and then put it in the fire. School picnics, family reunions, or club gatherings where the traditional bonfire is lit are wonderful opportunities for working fire magick. A bundle of herbs, fresh flowers, or small packets of incense can all be tossed on the fire as wish offerings. Before burning that pile of autumn leaves, inscribe a circle around it. On a small piece of paper, write out the negative influences you want to be rid of. Place the paper in the center of the pile. As the leaves burn, the negative influences are consumed in the flames.

Use your imagination. Think of how many ways you can incorporate magick into your daily life. See everything, every situation and place, as an opportunity to express your magickal ability.

12

Herbal Lore and Wisdom

Herbs are things of mystery, each a miracle of life itself,
experiencing growth, being, and reproduction.

—Paul Beyerl, *The Master Book of Herbalism*

Humans have always depended on the vegetative environment
for food, clothing, and shelter. Every culture has had its share of
shamans, wise women, and witch doctors: skillful individuals who
were able to heal the sick, manipulate the forces of nature, and
on occasion procure lovers for the lonely. Even today, when
modern medicine fails, those who practice alternative healing are
pursued for their guidance and wisdom.

Flowers, trees, and plants were so important to our ancestors
that many had their own myths and legends. It was said that the
goddess Athena invented the olive tree as a gift for her city of
Athens. The lily of the valley sprang from the tears of a virgin.
The Creator Sun God of Egypt rose from the primeval Lotus. In
the Middle Ages, there was a legend about a secret race of plant
men called mandrakes. These evil creatures apparently lived in
the forests and ate human flesh.

Then there is the ritualistic use of herbs, which has always been an integral part of sacred and magickal traditions. Herbal mixtures were, and still are, used for incense to lift the spirits, as hallucinogens to aid shamanic journeys, and as lures for the fulfillment of special desires. Today, Witches and healers still use herbs to protect their homes, heal sick friends, and aid them in their magickal works.

Along with their physical and medicinal qualities, plants also contain a subtle energy which can be tapped into. This energy is enhanced through the use of ritual or from strong intentions projected into the plant. Once a plant has been magickally charged, it will then actively attract or repel incoming vibrations as designated. Because of their life force and energy, plants make wonderful psychic conductors and especially powerful talismans.

Working With Herbs

Herbs provide us with an abundance of medicinal, as well as magickal, substances. Most herbs are easily grown and nurtured, because in reality they are weeds. Herbs will grow in the shade and between rocks, thrive in sandy soil, and can go for long periods of time without water. Once planted, herbs return year after year and serve as a useful as well as decorative ground cover.

Herb gardening is very nurturing and comforting, because it allows time for meditation and reflection—not to mention that once the herbs are harvested, they supply their caretaker with a bounty of magickal substances. Mysterious incenses, enchanting oils, fragrant sachets, delectable foods, and medicinal remedies are the rewards of herbal gardening.

There are many designs and varieties of herb gardens. The only limitation is your imagination. Whether you are a city dweller or country farmer, herbs can be your friends. There is no reason to want when it comes to Mother Nature. Herbs, flowers, and small trees all thrive on the patio, apartment balcony, kitchen windowsill, or in the well-lighted living room.

The following list will help you choose the best plants for your personal situation. Some herbs are better suited to large areas, and because of this will not do well in a window box. However, many of the smaller, and more delicate, varieties will thrive in hanging planters, strawberry pots, or in window gardens. Be sure to check with your neighborhood nursery or garden center to find out what varieties are best suited for your location.

The Magickal Properties of Plants and Herbs

The herbs which have been designated with an asterisk (★) will thrive in window boxes, strawberry pots, and hanging planters as long as they have plenty of light.

Acacia: Psychic power and protection.
Burn acacias to stimulate psychic power. It is also believed to protect against psychic attack and bad dreams when hung over a bed.

Alfalfa: Prosperity.
Alfalfa is used in money spells. When it is hung over a door or placed in a jar in the kitchen, it is believed to protect a household from poverty.

Angelica: Protection.
Angelica is used to protect a household from ghosts and hexes. When it is tied and hung, or added to bath water, it is said to remove curses and jinxes.

Angelica

Aster: Love.
The plant of good fortune and love. An aster can be carried, or added to spells, amulets, and charms to attract love.

★*Balm* (lemon): Love and success.
The balm is mixed wine for seduction spells. It can also be carried to attract love and success.

Balm, lemon

Barley: Love and protection.

When barley is scattered on the ground, it is believed to keep evil away. The Greeks made a drink of barley and water which was used during ritual to protect the participants from evil influences and warring factions.

★*Basil:* Love and protection.

Believed to ensure fertility. Basil makes a great love charm when administered in the food of a lover. It can also be carried in a bag to protect against hexes.

Basil

★*Borage:* Courage and psychic power.

Drink borage tea to increase psychic power. Crumbled borage can be placed in a pocket, or amulet pouch, for courage and psychic awareness.

Cardamom: Lust and love.

The seeds are ground and added to wine for love and lust spells. The cardamom pods are ground and added to love-drawing incense, or they can be carried whole as a love charm.

★*Carnation:* Healing and protection.

The flowers are worn to protect against hexes and black magick spells. Red carnations are placed in a sick room to aid in the healing process, and are placed near the windows to keep out negativity.

Carnation

★*Clover:* Luck, money, protection, and success.

Four-leaf clovers bring good luck. A red clover carried in some red flannel is said to keep evil away. Four sprigs of fresh clover tied with green ribbon are said to bring wealth.

Corn: Fertility, prosperity, and luck.

Corn is hung by the door or hearth to ensure the fertility of a household through the winter months. It is also believed that the first corn picked, when placed in a jar with silver coins, will bring wealth.

★Daisy: Lust and love.

Pick the first daisy in spring and love and good luck will come to you. Press the first daisy you pick in the spring, wrap it in pink and yellow silk, and good luck will follow you for the year.

Dandelion: Wishes and clairvoyance.

Drink dandelion wine to increase clairvoyance for divination. Blow all the fuzz off the dandelion into the wind as you make a wish and it will come true.

★Dill: Lust, love, and prosperity.

Dill is considered to be an aphrodisiac when mixed with food and wine. Place dill seeds in a green pouch and carry it for prosperity. When dill is added to a bath, it is said to make the bather irresistible.

Dill

Dogwood: Wishes and protection.

Place a flowering sprig of dogwood in the house for protection. Write out a wish on a piece of virgin parchment paper and bury it beneath a dogwood tree. When the dogwood flowers, the wish will come true.

Elecampane: Love and protection.

Make a pouch of red flannel, then fill it with elecampane leaves and dill seeds, and carry it to attract love. Burn elecampane leaves as an incense to drive out evil influences.

Fennel: Protection.

Fennel added to incense will protect a home against negativity. Fennel seeds carried in the pocket will protect one from harm.

★Fern: Health, wealth, and honor.

Fennel

Ferns make great house plants. It is said they will protect a household against negativity and poverty. Fern seeds are carried to gain the respect of others.

★Feverfew: Protection.

For protection carry feverfew flowers in a blue bag. Mix feverfew flowers in with your bath water before going out to protect your body against harm.

★Gardenia: Peace, love, and spirituality.

When a woman wears gardenias in her hair, she will attract love. Place gardenia petals on the floor of a house for peace; gardenia incense is burned to increase spiritual awareness.

★Garlic: Protection.

It is believed that when garlic is hung in the windows it will protect those inside against evil and the terrors of the night. Garlic can also be carried in the pocket for personal protection and good luck.

Garlic

Goldenrod: Prosperity and divination.

For prosperity, wrap goldenrod in a dollar bill and place it in a gold pouch. For psychic awareness, place a vase of fresh goldenrod on the table when doing card readings.

★Horehound: Healing and protection.

Carry a piece of horehound to guard against evil sorcery. Drink horehound tea to strengthen mental awareness.

Goldenrod

★Heather: Luck.

White heather is carried for good luck. Keep a heather plant in a house to attract positive energy.

★Hyssop: Purification.

Use hyssop as an aspergillum to sprinkle holy water when cleansing a room. Hang hyssop in the corners of the room to clear out negativity. Use hyssop in the bath to cleanse the body of negative energies.

Hyssop

Jasmine: Love and Money.

Jasmine flowers are added to incense and tea to attract love. They are also burned on charcoal to attract money. It is believed that when you carry three white jasmine flowers next to your cash it will increase.

Lavender: Love, protection, and happiness. Lavender perfume has long been used to attract love. Lavender placed in the drawers with clothes will protect the wearer. Lavender flowers are added to incense to bring peaceful sleep.

Lavender

Marigold: Money, prosperity, and success. Marigold petals are added to incense for prosperity. They can also be carried in a gold pouch for personal success.

Mint: Money and healing. Mint leaves will help relieve a headache when rubbed on the brow and temples. Mint tea will soothe an upset stomach. To increase cash flow, carry mint leaves in your wallet.

Marigold

Mugwort: Psychic power and astral projection. Sleep on a pillow filled with mugwort for prophetic dreams, or burn it as an incense to increase psychic power and aid astral projection.

Pansy: Love. Pansies are the plant of the heart. They are worn or carried for love and friendship. Pansies placed on the table during dinner will arouse the passions of love.

Parsley: Lust and protection. When eaten, parsley is said to promote fertility and feelings of love. It is also believed that when parsley is kept in the window, evil will not enter.

Patchouly: Money and fertility. Patchouly leaves are sprinkled in the purse, wallet and pocket to ensure wealth. Patchouly can be added to love oils, incenses, and baths to attract love.

Pea: Money and love.
Place six dried peas in a pouch with Irish moss to attract money. Chant the name of your desire when shelling peas, and he or she will soon appear.

Pennyroyal: Strength and protection.
Wear pennyroyal in a small bag around the neck to protect against the evil eye. Drinking pennyroyal tea will help to strengthen the resolve.

Pennyroyal

Rhubarb: Fidelity.
Serve rhubarb pie to a loved one to keep them faithful, and for deep and lasting love, add strawberries to the pie.

★Rose: Love, healing, and psychic power.
A single red rose is given for love, a pink rose for friendship, and a yellow rose for forgiveness. Carry a red silk bag filled with red rose petals to attract love.

★Rosemary: Love, lust, protection, and purification.
Send a sprig of rosemary tied with a pink ribbon to a loved one so they will remember you always. Add fresh rosemary to ritual incense to cleanse and purify an area, and place rosemary under a pillow for a peaceful sleep.

Rosemary

★Sage: Wisdom and protection.
A wreath made with sprigs of sage, rosemary, and thyme hung on a door will protect a household. Small pouches of sage can be carried, or worn around the neck, for wisdom.

★Savory: Healing and mental power.
Juice from the plant brings relief from bee stings. Savory carried in a pouch and sniffed will help clear mental confusion.

Sage

★Snapdragon: Protection.
Plant snapdragons around the border of a house to ward off evil. Place vases of snapdragons in the windows or in front of mirrors to repel negativity.

Star Anise: Psychic power.
Powdered star anise added to incense will increase psychic awareness. Gamblers believe that if they carry star anise seeds in their pockets it will bring them good luck.

★Sunflower: Wishes, health, and good fortune.
Dry the petals of the sunflower and add them to incense for good fortune. Plant sunflowers near a house to bring prosperity to a household. Make a wish and plant a sunflower; when it blooms the wish will come true.

Thistle: Protection and hex breaking.
Thistles sprinkled in the path of an enemy will cause them misfortune. Plant thistles near the front door of a house to protect it.

★Thyme: Love, courage, and healing.
Wear thyme in an amulet around the neck for good health. Women who wear thyme are said to be irresistible.

★Tulip: Prosperity and love.
Tulips in a house bring good fortune and prosperity. It is said that the first tulip of spring will bring love to the one who picks it.

Vervain: Protection, purification, and love.
When vervain is sprinkled around a room, it will protect all those who reside therein. If it is carried in a locket or hung in a pouch around the neck, it will protect the wearer from evil influences.

Thyme

Vervain

★Violet: Luck, love, and peace.

Mix violet flowers with lavender buds to create a love-drawing amulet. Violets are grown and given to friends for good luck and peace.

Wax Plant: Protection.

Keep a wax plant in a house, especially the bedroom, for protection against negative thoughts and vibrations. Dry the flowers and add to amulets for protection.

★Woodruff: Money, protection, and love.

When woodruff is added to May wine, it is said to bring good luck and love to all who drink it.

Woodruff

ELEMENTAL CORRESPONDENCES FOR PLANTS AND HERBS LISTED

North (Earth)	East (Air)	South (Fire)	West (Water)
Alfalfa	Acacia	Angelica	Aster
Barley	Borage	Basil	Balm, lemon
Corn	Clover	Carnation	Cardamom
Dogwood	Dandelion	Dill	Daisy
Fern	Elecampane	Fennel	Feverfew
Horehound	Goldenrod	Garlic	Gardenia
Mugwort	Lavender	Hyssop	Heather
Pea	Mint	Marigold	Jasmine
Patchouly	Parsley	Pennyroyal	Pansy
Rhubarb	Sage	Rosemary	Rose
Tulip	Savory	Snapdragon	Sunflower
Vervain	Star Anise	Thistle	Thyme
Wheat	Wax Plant	Woodruff	Violet

Harvesting Herbs

The best time to harvest herbs is in the summer and early fall. Those grown for their flowers should be cut and dried before the flower wilts. Seeds should always be picked when they appear and root herbs should be left until their tops die. In some cases, as with mint and basil, you will get more than one harvest. These plants should be pruned on a regular basis to promote fuller and healthier growth.

Remember, plants are living things and should be treated with respect. Always harvest herbs in such a way as not to deplete or inhibit future growth and development. Unless it is the final harvest, never take more than a third of the plant, and always pick where there is abundant and luxuriant growth. These herbs will posses the greatest strength and healing power.

First shake the dirt off the plant, and then carefully wash it in cool water. Gently shake the plant to get all of the water off of it. Then spread the plant out on a paper towel to absorb any remaining moisture. When the plant is thoroughly clean and dry, tie it with string and hang it in a well-ventilated room. Drying time will vary according to location and temperature.

Once the herbs have dried, crumble and place them in opaque, airtight containers. Label each container with the name of the herb and the date on which it was harvested. Culinary herbs like basil, chives, and sage can be frozen while still green. Freezing them preserves their fresh color and taste.

The Magick of Incense

Incense, like music, speaks without words to the conscious mind. It stirs the emotions as it brings back memories of things, events, places, and people long forgotten. Because of its evocative nature, incense has always played an important role in both religion and magic.

FRAGRANT HERBS, SPICES, AND WOODS

Because of their fragrance, the following herbs, spices, and woods smell lovely when burned alone.

Allspice berries *(spicy)*: Use for money, luck, and healing.
Bay leaves *(mellow)*: Use for protection and purification.
Calamus root *(sweet, fruity)*: Use for luck and money.
Cassia bark *(cinnamonlike)*: Use for love, protection, and psychic power.
Cedarwood *(mellow)*: Use for purification and protection.
Cloves *(warm, spicy)*: Use for love, protection, and money.
Deer's tongue leaves *(sweet, woodsy)*: Use for lust and psychic power.
Eucalyptus *(camphorlike)*: Use for healing and protection.
Fir needles *(sweet, pinelike)*: Use for fertility, protection, and money.
Lavender flowers *(flowery)*: Use for love, protection, and happiness.
Marjoram *(herby)*: Use for love, money, and happiness.
Myrtle leaves *(eucalyptuslike)*: Use for love, fertility, and money.
Orris root *(violetlike)*: Use for love, lust, and attraction.
Patchouly leaves *(musky)*: Use for love, money, and fertility.
Pine needles *(pine)*: Use for healing, money, and protection.
Rosemary *(heady, medicinal)*: Use for love, lust, and protection.
Sage *(herby)*: Use for wisdom and protection.
Sandalwood *(rich, mysterious)*: Use for protection, wishes, and spirituality.
Star Anise *(spicy)*: Use for psychic power and luck.
Thyme *(sweet, woodsy)*: Use for love, courage, and healing.
Tonka beans *(vanillalike)*: Use for love, luck, and attraction.
Vetivert *(rich, sensual)*: Use for lust, love, and money.

Priests and magicians have long believed that the burning of incense will attract higher spiritual forces. It is believed that incense has the ability to deliver prayers and wishes, spoken into its smoke, directly to the realm of the gods. These prayers are then blessed and their petitioner's wishes are granted.

Essentially, incense can be made from any substance as long as it smells good when burned. Some of the more traditional ingredients used are spices like clove and cinnamon, woods like sandalwood and aloes, and resins such as frankincense and myrrh. The reason these aromatic substances smell so good is because of their essential oil, which is volatilized by heat-emitting perfumed smoke.

How to Make Magickal Incense

Incense comes in two forms: combustible, which is in the form of cones, sticks, and blocks; and noncombustible, which comes in the form of powder or resin. The simplest kind of incense to make is the noncombustible kind, which does not require mucilage or an ignitable substance. Noncombustible incense is also far less messy and frustrating to deal with.

The base for noncombustible incense is generally talcum powder and/or sawdust and/or powdered spice, to which saltpeter is added to make it burn. A powerful essential oil is then added for fragrance, along with a dye for color. The incense is then burned in a censer on small church charcoal blocks.

To create your own magickal incenses, begin with a base, talcum, sawdust, or special spice blend. Add the appropriate herbs or resins to the base and grind the mixture into a powder, then add a few drops of perfume or essential oil. Mix well to blend the oil and powder together. Place the incense in a jar with a tightly fitting lid and label accordingly.

Magickal Incense Blends

The following formulas are for noncombustible incense. You will need a grinder, a small mixing bowl, an eye dropper, measuring spoons, and jars for storage. Grind all of the herbal ingredients into a fine powder, add the oil, and mix thoroughly. Store in glass jars or plastic bags.

Try to time your incense making to the appropriate cycle of the moon. For love and attraction, use the new to full moon; personal or psychic power uses the full moon; and for protection or banishing, use the waning moon.

Before you begin to make any magickal substance, take a few moments to think about what you are doing and why. As you blend the ingredients together, firmly instill your intent into the mixture. Visualize your desire, and audibly chant or speak this desire as you work, forcing it into the very essence of the incense. This extra effort of focused energy will enhance the incense, and the magickal work it is intended for.

INCENSE RECIPES

Love-Drawing Incense

1 part sandalwood base
1 part lavender buds
1/2 tsp. basil
3 drops rose oil
1 drop lavender oil
color red or pink

Lust-Drawing Incense

1 part sandalwood base
1 part dragon's blood powder
1/2 part lavender buds
1/2 part orris root powder
3 drops musk oil
3 drops rose oil
1 drop cherry oil
color red

Prosperity Incense

2 parts frankincense sittings
1 part cassia chips
1 part orange peel
1 part allspice
3 drops orange spice oil
2 drops cinnamon oil
1 drop myrrh oil

Money-Drawing Incense

2 parts talcum base
1 part cassia chips
1 part crushed allspice
1 part frankincense
1 part marigold petals
3 drops frankincense oil
2 drops clove oil
color green

Protection Incense

2 parts talcum base
2 parts patchouly
2 parts sandalwood
3 drops patchouly oil
3 drops sandalwood oil
3 drops sage oil
color black

High Altar Incense

2 parts frankincense
2 parts myrrh
2 parts copal drops
3 drops myrrh oil
2 drops ambergris oil

Full Moon Incense

2 parts orris root powder
2 parts lavender buds
2 parts myrrh powder
2 parts calamus
3 drops jasmine oil
3 drops rose oil
3 drops gardenia oil

Success Incense

2 parts sandalwood base
2 parts marigold petals
2 parts red storax
2 parts juniper berries
3 drops carnation oil
3 drops ambergris oil
3 drops frankincense oil
1 pinch of saffron

Magickal Oils

The blending of magickal oils is simple and requires little equipment other than an eye dropper, essential oils, and small bottles for storage. If you wish to create your own special blend, be sure the ingredients complement each other and reflect your desired goal. To enhance the effectiveness of your oil add a crystal, semiprecious stone, flower, seed, or leaf to the bottle. Always be sure to label the bottle according to its purpose and date of creation.

STANDARD MAGICKAL OILS

Love-Drawing Oil

1 pair of Adam and Eve roots
1 part rose oil
1 part cherry oil
1 part musk oil
1 part narcissus oil

Money-Drawing Oil

2 parts apricot oil base
2 parts cinnamon oil
2 parts clove oil
2 parts frankincense oil
1 small High John root in bottle

Power Oil

2 parts safflower oil
2 parts sandalwood oil
2 parts orange oil
2 parts pine oil
2 parts blue sonata
1 garnet
1 ruby

Desire Me Oil

2 parts white musk oil
2 parts jasmine oil
2 parts lotus oil
2 parts violet oil
1 rose quartz in bottle

Crown of Success Oil

2 parts sunflower oil
2 parts orange oil
2 parts allspice oil
2 parts ambergris oil
Add gold glitter to bottle

Protection Oil

2 parts patchouly oil
2 parts sandalwood oil
2 parts frankincense oil
2 parts verbena oil
1 onyx chip
1 wormwood leaf or stem

Thoughts and Ideas

Since ecology and holistic healing have become household words, the availability of fresh herbs and plants has increased. Almost every city, large or small, has its share of health food stores and nutrition centers. Even grocery stores have jumped on the bandwagon, and now carry a variety of fresh roots and herbs. And, for those who wish to purchase ready-made products, there are a large number of mail order companies from which to choose.

When requesting a catalog from any mail order company, it is always wise to enclose a self-addressed stamped envelope. Some companies will send you their catalogs for free; others will charge for them. If the company charges for their catalog, your money is usually refunded with your first purchase. The companies listed below deal in a variety of herbs, essential oils, and ready-made incenses, as well as other supplies.

MoonScents and Magical Blends
P.O. Box 381588
Cambridge, MA 02238
(800) 368-7417

Aphrodisia
282 Bleeker St.
New York, NY 10018
212-989-6440

Eye of the Day
P.O. Box 21261
Boulder, CO 80308
(800) 717-3307

World Wide Curio House
P.O. Box 17095
Minneapolis, MN 55417
(no telephone orders)

The Excelsior Incense Works
1413 Van Dyke Ave.
San Francisco, CA 94124
(800) 423-1125

13

Treasures From the Earth

Quartz crystals are the manifestation of the Creator's finest hour of expression. They are windows of light with many facets which show the myriad dimensions of life created from cosmic dust in an ever expanding universe.

—Randall N. Baer, *Windows of Light*

From the earliest times, gemstones, especially crystals, have fascinated humankind. Beyond their outward beauty, crystals are reservoirs of power. They have an energy which can be directed toward healing, used for protection, or to stimulate spiritual awareness. Once they have been magickally charged, crystals can help focus and direct personal power toward desired goals.

There are many different kinds of crystals, but of them all, quartz is the master gemstone. It can be found throughout the world and is especially noted for its healing qualities.

Quartz crystal is composed of silicon and oxygen (SiO_2) which is considered to be the building block of minerals. In fact, most of our planet is composed of minerals containing SiO_2. Silicon dioxide is also an important constituent of the human body, which may be the physical basis for our connection to crystals.

Crystals are formed clear, like frozen water, and only change color when other minerals are introduced into their structure. It is this addition of other minerals, such as iron and magnesium, which produces rose quartz, yellow quartz, and amethyst.

The quartz crystal is one of the earth's most used minerals. It has been used to amplify sound in a loudspeaker, microphone, and other audio equipment. In watches and clocks, quartz helps synchronize time. Quartz crystal has also been used to direct energy in laser technology and transmit whole-spectrum light in optical lenses.

In Witchcraft and magick, quartz crystals are used as luck charms, protection talismans, love amulets, and as healing agents. They are also used in conjunction with various planets and constellations of the zodiac to enhance ritual effectiveness. No matter how they are used, crystals help magnify and extend personal energy and power.

The wonderful thing about working with crystals is that they have the ability to reinforce and sustain human energy vibrations. When this happens, the physical body is strengthened as well as rejuvenated. This can be very helpful, especially when the individual is involved in a lengthy or physically demanding situation.

The purchasing of a crystal or gemstone should be done carefully. For personal use, as in jewelry, it is best to select crystals and stones according to their size, cut, and clarity. However, when choosing a crystal or gemstone for ritual work, its magickal qualities should be considered over its physical appearance. Certainly, the ultimate criteria in the selection process will depend on how the stone or crystal *feels* to you.

The Magickal Values of Crystals and Gemstones

Agate comes in a variety of colors and is used for strength, courage, victory, and alignment with earth energies. It can be worn to protect against gossip, as a truth amulet, and to ensure favors from powerful people. Use agate to build personal strength and courage.

Amber is a highly prized, fossilized resin, which was a favorite among the ancients. Amber is solar fire, the congealed rays of the setting sun. It is worn for strength, protection, beauty, and love.

Amethyst is purple quartz and spiritual in nature. A very popular stone among Witches. Amethyst is used to clear confusion, aid in prophetic dreams, and protect against self-deception. Use amethyst during meditation to help clear up issues of a spiritual nature.

Aquamarine, sometimes called sea water, belongs to the goddess of the ocean. It is a pale blue-green color and is carried to enhance psychic power. The stone is also used for healing, purification, and to bring love and happiness.

Bloodstone is green in color and flecked with red spots. It is associated with the blood and has the ability to stop bleeding. Bloodstone is worn for protection against physical injury. Carried for good luck, protection, money, and business.

Carnelian, red-orange in color, is warm and smooth to touch. The stone is carried for courage and to halt jealousy and envy. It is also believed that carnelian will prevent certain skin diseases. Use for protection, healing, courage, and sexual energy.

Cat's-eye is a luminous stone, olive green or amber in color. It is worn or carried to increase beauty and preserve youth. Cat's-eye is also used in money spells and to bring luck in gambling.

Crystal Quartz this master power stone, is associated with both Fire and Water because it has the ability to focus the sun's energy rays to ignite wood chips or other combustible material and resembles solidified water or ice. Witches wear crystals to represent the Goddess, the moon, and psychic power. Crystals are used for protection, healing, and power.

Diamond, like the quartz crystal, is prized for its clarity and brilliance. Diamonds are associated with the sun, the element of fire, and the ability to resonate energy. Wear or carry diamonds for protection, courage, wealth, peace, sexual energy, spiritual enlightenment, health, and strength.

Emerald is a brilliant green stone and one of the most expensive on the market. It is associated with the goddess Venus and the element of earth. The emerald is used in love spells, rituals dealing with monetary gain, and to increase mental powers.

Garnet bright red and fiery, is worn to bestow faithfulness and friendship. The garnet is associated with Mars and the ability to protect, heal, and enhance bodily strength. Use the garnet for protection, healing, strength, friendship, and love.

Jade is a sacred stone in China, where it is placed on altars to the sun and moon. Jade is also associated with Venus and worn to attract love and marriage. Jade is green in color and can be used for love, healing, longevity, wisdom, and to prolong life.

Jet is a fossilized wood, millions of years old. Beads of jet are worn along with amber by Witches for protection, psychic power, good luck, and health.

Lapis Lazuli, prized by the ancient Egyptians for its royal blue color and flecks of golden pyrite, is associated with Venus and Mars. It is used to bring joy, love, friendship, courage, and to protect against infidelity.

Moonstone is an opalescent blue or white feldspar. The moonstone has long been associated with the goddess of the moon. It is worn or carried for love, divination, protection, youth, and healing. Most Witches prize the moonstone above all others because of its connection to the Goddess.

Onyx, a black stone associated with Saturn, is worn for protection, defense against negative forces, to reduce sexual desire, and to enhance magickal operations.

Rhodocrosite, a beautiful pink stone, gives off a loving and warm vibration. Rhodocrosite is worn to enhance beauty, to build friendships, and to attract love. It can also be used to reduce stress and fatigue.

Ruby has long been considered the stone of Buddha. The ruby is associated with Mars, the element of fire, and is highly prized for its vivid red color. Rubies are worn or carried for protection, personal power, joy, attraction, wealth, and spirituality.

Sapphire is a very powerful and spiritual stone. It is associated with the god Apollo and is worn to stimulate the third eye. The sapphire is worn or carried for love, meditation, peace magick, power, and to enhance spiritual activity.

Topaz is used to bring wealth. This lovely yellow-gold stone is associated with the sun, fire, and the Egyptian god Ra. Topaz can be used for protection, healing, or attracting money and great wealth.

Turquoise, favored by many North American Indian tribes for its beauty and healing qualities, is associated with the goddess Venus, the element of earth and the Great Spirit. Turquoise is used for healing, courage, money, protection, friendship, and is said to bring the wearer good fortune.

Working With Crystals and Gem Stones

Crystals and gemstones, by virtue of their contrasting crystalline structures, have different properties and energies associated with them. These energies can be tapped by wearing jewelry set with certain crystals or stones, carrying them in pouches, or using them during meditation and magick. It is also possible to channel energy through a crystal onto a specific area of the body to aid in healing.

Working with stones and crystals is a direct experience with energy as it moves from moment to moment. There is no way to really "know about" working with crystals in the sense of developing standard techniques which can be learned and applied to everyone. Each individual is unique and different, and so is their energy output. When working with crystals or stones, it is the energy output of the individual handling the crystal which produces the final outcome.

Learning to work with minerals is easy. Begin by experimenting with a single quartz crystal. Choose one small enough to carry but large enough to work with. In addition to size, clarity and perfection of the crystal should be considered—make sure your crystal is reasonably clear and free of chips and scratches.

Once you have selected a crystal to work with, you will need to cleanse and charge it. Cleansing the crystal will remove any previous thoughts and vibrations which may be on it. Charging the crystal will program it with your thoughts and vibrations.

There are many different ways to cleanse a crystal; four of them are presented here. Read through each process and choose the one you feel most comfortable with. Use this method to clean and charge all new crystals and stones you acquire. Try to choose one system and stick with it, since consistency is an important part of developing magickal power.

Crystals pick up and temporarily hold charges radiating from exterior sources. Negative thought-forms and emotions, electronic pollution, inharmonious sounds, and imbalanced electromagnetic energies can all affect the vibratory energy of your crystal. If the dissonant energies are not cleaned off the crystal's surface, it may crack or develop inclusions. Consequently, it is important to cleanse your crystals on a regular basis to keep them functioning at their optimum effectiveness.

Crystal Cleansing

The following items will be needed to clean a crystal: sea salt, an empty bowl, an incense burner or smudge pot, charcoal and matches, a smudging stick or loose smudge incense, and a protective pouch to hold the crystal when carried.

Place your crystal in the empty bowl and cover it with salt. Place the bowl where it will receive full sunlight and moonlight for three days. On the fourth day, remove the crystal from the salt and rinse it in cool water. Light the smudge stick or smudge incense. Hold the crystal in the smoke emanating from the incense as you chant the following:

All negative thoughts are banished
All unwanted vibrations are gone.
Only the forces and powers I wish
Shall be with me from this moment on!

Repeat this process for about a minute or until you are sure that the crystal is clean and free of negative vibrations.

This second method is very simple and effective because it involves the natural cleansing power of the earth. First, place your crystal in a bowl of salt for twenty-four hours. When the time period has elapsed, remove the crystal from the salt, wrap it in cheesecloth and tie with a white cord. Take the wrapped crystal to the nearest fresh-water stream or to the ocean. Place the crystal in the water but secure it to a branch or rock so it will not drift away. Leave it in the water for three to four hours. Retrieve your crystal, unwrap it, and place it a protective bag. It is now ready to program with your thoughts and vibrations.

For this third cleansing method, you will need a crystal cluster twice the size of the crystal you plan to cleanse. First cleanse the cluster using one of the previous methods. Once the cluster has been cleansed, place it in a window where it will get direct sunlight for a good portion of the day. Allow the cluster to absorb direct sunlight for three days before using it to clean other crystals.

When you use the cluster for cleaning, you must first wash the crystal you intend to clean in salt water. Without drying the crystal, place it on the cluster in full sunlight. Leave it for twenty-four hours and the cluster will clean the crystal for you.

This fourth procedure for cleansing crystals is one of the most popular. To do it you will need either a smudge stick or loose smudging herbs,[1] a smudge pot or a fireproof dish, charcoal if you're using a loose herb mixture, and a smudge fan.

---

[1]Smudge mixture is made from equal parts: sage, cedar, and lavender; sage, copal, and cedar; or sweet grass and sage. Smudge sticks are prepackaged and can be purchased in most New Age book stores, from occult supply houses, or American Indian shops.

Prior to smudging, wash your crystal in salt water. Place the items you are going to use on your altar, or on a small table covered with a white cloth. Light the smudge stick. If you are using smudge herbs, light the charcoal and sprinkle the herbs directly on it. When the smudge begins to smolder, fan the smoke in an upward direction. Hold your crystal in the center of the smoke as you chant the following:

> *Herbs of the earth*
> *Crystal of power,*
> *Be thou cleansed*
> *From this hour.*

Crystal Programming

After a crystal has been properly cleansed, it should be programmed for personal use. This is a simple process which imbeds personal feelings and desires deep within the heart of the crystal. Once programmed, a crystal becomes a unique magickal tool attuned to its owner's individual vibratory frequency.

Programming a crystal for personal use is easily done. Think of your crystal as a mini-computer, and what you program into it designates what it will be able to do. The thought-forms used to energize the crystal will determine the power and frequency level at which it will vibrate. If you program the crystal with love, it will radiate love. Conversely, if you program it with determination, aggressiveness, and force, these will be the vibrations it will emit.

Crystals attract and hold energy vibrations, which makes them useful tools for focusing and directing energy. Once a crystal has been cleaned, it is ready to be programmed for personal use. Of the many ways available to program a crystal, the following two methods are the most common.

Hold the crystal in your hand and create a thought-form of what you want to happen. For example, if you want to program the crystal for good health, visualize yourself energetic and in glowing health. You will then need to force this vision or thought-form into the crystal. To intensify the visualization, chant or speak your desire directly into the crystal.

The other way to program a crystal involves holding it over your heart. Form a mental picture (thought-form) of your desire and allow this picture to flow directly from your heart into the crystal. To empower the mental picture, reaffirm it audibly through a prayer or chant.

Crystals and Atlantis

It is believed that the major source of power in ancient Atlantis came from crystals. Large symmetrical crystals known as generators were precision cut and highly polished. Their quality was flawless, as was their ability to refract, hold, and transfer light energy. In addition to being a source of energy, crystals were also used in Atlantean libraries. The libraries imprinted their documents on flat crystals known as record keepers. The record keeper was then held by the reader and the vibrations it emitted were interpreted psychically.

For the most part, communication in Atlantean times was psychic in nature. Crystals were used in schools to teach students how to focus, amplify, and transmit their thoughts without the need to vocalize. They were also taught how to use energy to move and relocate physical objects. Unfortunately, greed and misuse of crystal technology led to the destruction of the Atlantean civilization.

The following ritual employs some of the same principles that were used in Atlantis to energize crystals. The objective is to use a large generator crystal to empower smaller stones and crystals with healing energy. When your smaller stones or crystals weaken and lose their magnetism, they can be recharged through the ritual. (You'll notice they've lost their energy when they look dull and dirty, and they no longer feel energized.)

The Atlantean Crystal Ritual

For this ritual you will need a light box,[2] a generator crystal, the crystal you want to charge, and your customary magickal

Generator Crystal

accessories. The generator crystal has six natural facets which join sharply together to form the terminated apex. The crystal is supported by six sides, and usually cloudy near the base and clear at the top. Generator crystals teach us how to concentrate, focus, and direct energy.

The generator crystal is placed on top of the light box in the center of the altar. The light in the box is turned on and the generator crystal is covered with a dark cloth. On the altar, in addition to the generator, there will be two white candles, smudge incense, a fan, a bowl of salt and one of water, and the athame for casting the circle.

Suggested Altar Setup for the Atlantean Crystal Ritual

---

[2]A light box is a large square box with a hole in the center. A small light bulb is attached to the inside and can be turned on and off with a switch attached to the cord. When the box is lit, anything placed on top of it will glow. Light boxes can be found in most New Age stores where crystals are sold.

The Ritual

To begin the ritual, light the right altar candle and then the left altar candle as follows:

I call upon the forces fiery and bright.
I call upon the forces of power and might.

Cast away the shadows, bring in the light
That will ever guard and guide me this night.

Light the smudge and fan the smoke around the entire area in which you will be working as you say:

All negative thoughts are banished
All unwanted vibrations are gone.
Only the forces and powers I wish
Shall be with me from this moment on!

Replace the smudge and fan on the altar and pick up the bowl of salt. Take three pinches of salt and put them into the bowl of water. Walking in a deosil direction, sprinkle the water and salt mixture on the ground around your working area as you say:

Earth and water now combine
To create this holy shrine
None shall enter without my grace
For this now is my sacred space

Return to the altar and place the bowl back on it. At this point you will want to cast your magick circle around the area in which you are going to be working. After the circle has been cast, stand and face the generator crystal and say:

Delightful was the land beyond dreams
Fairer than aught mine eyes have ever seen

Where crystals lined sunlit shores
And death was known nevermore.
A land laden with prosperity
Where sweetened fruit adorned each tree
Atlantis was the time of power
Whose magick force I seek this hour.
None so great has since been known
Yet through my visions I am shown.
What can be done with these gifts of light
When used for what is good and right.

Now lift the cover off the crystal so that it shines brightly. Place the stones you wish to charge next to the generator crystal. Take a few moments to relax and focus on your intentions. When you feel the time is right, hold your hands palm down over the generator crystal and force all your energy into it as you chant:

With power and might
The crystal burns bright

Take a few moments to reflect or meditate on the ritual and your intentions. When a sufficient amount of time has passed, retrieve your stones and crystals from around the generator and cover it with the cloth. Extinguish the altar candles, beginning with the left, as you say:

Let now the forces of fire and light
And the magick of power and might,
Remain within, always burn bright
Ever to guard and guide me this night
So shall it be.

To bring to an end the Atlantean Crystal Ritual, take down the magick circle and put all items away.

Thoughts and Ideas

Crystals are bridges of light that serve to reflect individual consciousness. They are tools which help us focus and direct energy toward the manifestation of a goal. The key to crystal magick is in learning how to merge human awareness with crystal consciousness. When the human will is synthesized with the emanation of the crystal's energy, the resulting transition will contain both power and direction. By working with crystals, you learn how they respond in different situations. The knowledge you glean from your experiments can then be incorporated into magickal rites and spells. There is no doubt that the more you know about the natural elements of magick, the better Witch you will be.

Success Bag

This spell is especially good for attracting prosperity and personal success. Use it to get that all-important new job, promotion, or pay raise.

For this spell you will need the following items: one moss agate, one herkimer diamond, one pair of loadstones, one High John root, a gold satin or velvet bag, and six whole almonds painted gold. Once painted, the almonds should resemble gold nuggets.

Place all the items inside the bag, which should then be placed in a window or outside where it can receive direct sunlight most of the day. Leave the bag in the sun for six days. On the seventh day, retrieve it and chant the following over it six times:

> *Gifts of Earth, Fire, and stone*
> *Grant to me your power alone.*

Carry the bag with you when you and reaffirm its power by repeating the chant while visualizing your desire. Just before asking for that pay raise or promotion, hold the bag tightly and repeat the chant while visualizing your desire.

Self-Confidence Spell

Items needed for this spell are a piece of rose quartz and a pink candle. When you feel the need for more self-confidence and self-esteem, this simple ritual will help revitalize you.

First, relax and try to let go of your fears and tensions as you light the pink candle. Pick up the rose quartz, hold it in your hands, and feel the love and peace which emanates from it. Take several deep breaths and then, slowly, chant the following seven times:

> *Cosmic forces, above and below*
> *Come to my aid, and help me to know*
> *To find, to seek, to look within*
> *To overcome insecurities which creep in.*
> *I ask thee now to enter my dreams*
> *And fulfill my desires for self-esteem.*
> *May I now have confidence in all I do*
> *And all new goals now shine through.*
> *From this time on, I set forth in harmony*
> *Life, light, and love. As I will, so mote it be!*

Focus all your attention on the candle flame and concentrate on the chant. As you do this, feel your personal power and self-confidence grow and strengthen. Visualize yourself as a courageous and determined person who will achieve your goals and desires from this time forward. When you feel the time is right, extinguish the candle and carry the rose quartz with you.

Money-Drawing Spell

Items needed: a green cloth bag, a small pair of loadstones, a buckeye, and coins (one each, a penny, nickel, dime, and quarter), a gold candle, money-drawing incense, charcoal, matches, parchment paper, and pen.

On the first Sunday morning after the new moon before the hour of noon, place all the required items on your altar. Place the altar near a window where the sun will shine directly on it. Light some of the money-drawing incense and visualize money coming to you.

Next, pass all of the items on the table through the incense smoke as you chant the following:

A constant flow of cash I see
Is coming now, is coming to me.

Take a moment to visualize money coming to you.

Then light the gold candle and pass all of the items through it, chanting:

My financial needs will be fulfilled
From this moment on as I have willed.

Again visualize the amount of money you need coming to you).

At this time place all of the items, one at a time, into the green bag as you chant:

Money now flows directly to me
For this is my will, so mote it be.

Place the bag next to the candle and allow it to burn out. All the items should be left until the sun has set. After sunset, return your altar to its normal place, and the next time you leave the house, carry the bag with you.

14

Objects of Power and Dominion

A talisman is any object, sacred or profane, with or without appropriate inscriptions of symbols, uncharged or consecrated by means of appropriate ritual magic or meditation.

—Israel Regardie, *How to Make and Use Talismans*

Science has shown us that everything possesses an energy field which can be perceived by one of the human senses. We know that all living things and objects transmit vibrations, and that these vibrations communicate emotions and states of being. Though we may not fully understand how transmitted vibrations work, we do know they appeal to the unconscious or subconscious levels of human intelligence, and that they link us to our environment.

Every object and natural element has the potential of becoming a magickal link between the Witch and his or her objective. From a simple plastic charm to an elaborately carved fetish, all things are viewed as having magnetism. This inherent magnetism is then emphasized through magickal rites, when the powers laying dormant within the object are awakened. In Witchcraft, these magickally charged objects are referred to as talismans or amulets.

Once created, a talisman or amulet will emit a level of energy which can be used as a protection magnet, or to attract a principle force of a like nature. It is through correspondence linking,[1] and then the consecration of the object through ritual, that creates the talisman effect. Thus, for example, a love talisman might be made of copper, inscribed with the symbol for Venus, and consecrated on a Friday, the day sacred to Venus.

Some of the most popular talismans used today come from the grimoires penned by Renaissance ceremonial magicians. The source for many of these talismans' powers were the seven planets, the twelve signs of the zodiac, and their corresponding numerical configurations. In addition to astrological value, acclaimed magicians also placed emphasis on magickal squares, particular sigils, and hierarchical names. The appropriate name or symbol was engraved on a metal, wood, or stone disk, which was then consecrated and bequeathed to the needful recipient to work on his or her behalf.

Today, nearly all Witches and magicians make their own amulets and talismans, the reason being, it is the work and ingenuity which goes into the making of a magickal object that gives it its effectiveness. A true talisman is a custom-made artifact, usually designed for a specific purpose by the intended user. Most practitioners of the magickal arts will agree that amulets and talismans work best, and sometimes solely, for their maker.

The established meaning of the word *talisman* is "to consecrate." It is the process of consecration that converts a mundane object into an effective vehicle for inducing changes to occur in

---

[1]Correspondence linking is the bringing together, through the construction of an object, of archetypal energies by using specific materials, colors, numbers, designs, symbols, and/or angelic vibrations in conformity with the will of the magician.

accordance with the will. According to MacGregor Mathers[2] of the Golden Dawn, a talisman is "a magickal figure charged with the force it is intended to represent." A talisman should be constructed to attain a definite result. It is not like a charm or amulet, which is generally used for bringing good luck or warding off evil. An efficient talisman should be capable of operating in such a way so that its effectiveness is obvious immediately, or at least within seven days of its construction.

Talismans can be made to do all sorts of things: to acquire money, obtain patronage, recover lost property, influence people, obtain knowledge, disrupt friendships, compel someone to love you, and to protect your property and loved ones. The thing to remember about talismans is that once created and charged, they can be left to do their work—without further attention. This is because the energy set up by the operator continues to work over a set period of time. Talismans work like a battery and have the benefit of being self-recharging to some extent (if their construction has been carried out correctly). This recharging ability is due to the relationship between the talisman and its corresponding symbolic force.

Working With Talismans

Talismans always have been, and always will be, a central and integral part of the practice of Witchcraft. They provide the Witch with the ability to summon forth the cosmic powers of the universe. Along with amulets and charms, talismans make it possible for the Witch to extend, as well as intensify, his or her personal magnetism.

What makes the talisman such a powerful expression of magickal force is its occult symbolism. Ancient magickal seals such as those of Solomon, Moses, and David are full of not only original

[2]MacGregor Mathers was a ceremonial magician and author of related books, as well as the founder of the Golden Dawn magickal order.

power, but also of the power built into them through thousands of years of use. They also reflect the inner universe of human nature and its desire for control in accordance with will.

Talismans are created to help unlock the powers within us, as well as provide access to the powers outside of us. Talismans, seals, natural amulets, and carefully crafted charms are vehicles of magickal force. Tremendous hidden energy dwells within the heart of the well-constructed talisman, and it can be of great benefit to its owner.

In the making of a talisman you face several tasks. The first is to make, find, or buy an object properly suited to create the desired effect. You must then cleanse the object, or objects, of all previous thoughts and vibrations. Finally, you must construct the talisman and then consecrate it to serve a specific purpose.

Traditional Cleansing Ritual

Everything you use in a magickal rite or spell should be cleansed of all previous thoughts and vibrations. This includes crystals and stones, planetary pentacles, seals, or handcrafted symbols. Containers such as boxes, bags, or bottles should also be purged of undesirable energies.

You can never be sure of what the previous owner experienced while in possession of your treasure. Even new, or personally handcrafted, items should be cleansed, because they may have been handled by an angry or unhappy individual. It is always best to start with a clean slate, so that there is nothing to interfere with your goal.

Cleansing Ritual

This ritual incorporates the power of the four elements to remove psychic impurities from most physical objects. Through the medium of elemental energy, impure thoughts (Air), hateful or aggressive actions (Fire), unhappy or bitter emotions (Water), and profane or temporal energies (Earth) are released. The spells which follow this cleansing ritual are designed to endow the object with a specified objective, thus turning the object into a talisman or amulet.

To perform this ritual you will need the following items:

Two white altar candles and standard altar equipment.
Sandalwood incense, placed on the East side of the altar.
One red candle, placed on the South side of the altar.
One bowl of water, placed on the West side of the altar.
One bowl of salt, placed on the North side of the altar.

Begin by consecrating the elements and casting the circle in the traditional manner.

Light the altar candles (right first, then the left) as you say the following:

> *Let now the powers of life and light*
> *Bless and protect me on this night.*

Light the incense on the East side of the altar as you say the following:

> *Let now the element of air bring forth insight and wisdom.*

Light the red candle on the South side of the altar as you say the following:

> *Let now the element of fire bring forth strength and power.*

Pick up the bowl of water on the West side of the altar and hold it in offering, as you say the following:

> *Let now the element of water bring forth control and dominion.*

Pick up the bowl of salt on the North side of the altar and hold it in offering, as you say the following:

> *Let now the element of earth guard and guide all my works.*
> *So shall it be.*

Pick up the object (amulet or talisman) you wish to cleanse, and pass it through the smoke of the incense as you say:

> *I cleanse thee with the element of air.*
> *Let all previous thoughts begone.*

Pass the object through the candle flame as you say:

> *I cleanse thee with the element of fire.*
> *Let all previous desires begone.*

Sprinkle the object with some water as you say:

> *I cleanse thee with the element of water.*
> *Let all previous emotions begone.*

Sprinkle the object with some salt as you say:

> *I cleanse thee with the element of earth.*
> *Let all previous vibrations begone.*

Now hold the object tightly, visualize any residual thoughts or energies leave the object, as you chant the following:

> *Elements of life, this charge I lay,*
> *No negativity in the presence stay.*
> *Hear my words addressed to thee,*
> *For as my word, so mote it be.*

Once the object has been cleansed, place it on the altar, take a few moments to reflect on what the object will be used for. When you feel the time is right extinguish the candles (first the left, then the right, and then the red one) chant as follows:

Let now the forces of power and might,
Ever burn long, ever burn bright,
Guide and guard me through the night.
That I shall walk in truth and light.
So mote it be.

Take down the circle in the usual manner. Keep the cleansed object, or objects, on your altar, or carefully stored until time for use.

Jupiter Prosperity Talisman Spell

Jupiter is the planet of expansion, idealism, and ambition. Jupiter is good to use for career success. situations concerned with money, legal transactions, and religious expansion. The following talisman will help you get a job, a raise in pay, collect a debt, or can be used in any situation where acquiring money is necessary.

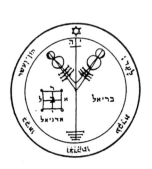

Jupiter Pentacle

Items needed: Jupiter Pentacle,[3] Jupiter incense,[4] fresh Jasmine flowers, an orange candle, small bottle of olive oil, a pin with which to write on the candle, charcoal, and matches.

[3]Pentacles can be found in the *Key of Solomon the King,* by MacGregor Mathers. York Beach, Maine.

[4]Jupiter incense: mix equal parts of ground anise, clove, and nutmeg, to which you add four drops of honeysuckle oil. Place an amethyst in the jar to enhance the magickal quality of the incense.

Three days before the full moon, bruise the jasmine flowers and place them in the bottle of olive oil. On the night of the full moon, place all of the items needed on your altar. When all is ready, take several deep breaths, relax, and clear your mind. You are then ready to begin. Light the incense as you say:

Let the spirit of Air grant me insight
and wisdom to accomplish my desire.

Relax, take a couple more deep breaths, and begin to visualize what it is you want or are trying to accomplish. Pick up the candle and carve your name on one side and your desire on the other. Now, as you visualize what you want, dress the candle with the oil while you chant the following:

Success and prosperity come to me
As I will, so mote it be!

Place the candle in the candleholder and light it. Again, visualize what it is you want. Pick up the Jupiter Pentacle, hold it in both hands, and chant the following (while raising as much energy as you can):

This talisman shall bring to me
Honor, wealth, and prosperity.
As I will, so mote it be!

Place the talisman under the candle. Allow the candle to burn for two hours. Repeat this spell for three more days. Each time you perform the spell, dress the candle with the oil and then allow it to burn for two hours. On the last day, let the candle burn out and then carry the talisman with you in your purse or pocket.

First Pentacle of the Sun Talisman Spell

The sun radiates light, energy, and hope. It bestows power and the ability to manifest desire in accordance with will. The sun brings forth life, and the positive nature of all things. The sovereignty of this solar planet encourages wealth, success, power, friendship, and patronage for business. All things are possible when the power of the sun is invoked.

First Pentacle of the Sun

The First Pentacle of the Sun from *The Greater Key of Solomon*[5] transmits the countenance of the Almighty, at whose aspect all creatures obey, and to the Angelic spirits to do reverence on bended knees. The face on the pentacle is that of the angel Metatron, one of the greatest of all angels, honored as the angel of presence, chief recording angel, chancellor of heaven, and the angel by whom the world is maintained.

To make this talisman you need to engrave the First Pentacle of the Sun onto a gold or brass disk, or onto heavy yellow construction paper.[6] In addition to the pentacle, you will need a small gold bag and some marigold seeds.

On the first Sunday after the new moon, take your pentacle and marigold seeds into the garden. If you do not have a garden, any secluded outdoor spot will do. Stand so that you are in the direct rays of the sun. Hold the pentacle and the seeds so that the rays of the sun shine directly on them. Charge them with the following Prosperity Chant:

---

[5] *The Greater Key of Solomon*, L. W. de Laurence, Scott and Co. 1914.

[6] When you make talismans on paper it is a good idea to laminate them for protection.

Almighty One of wealth and power,
Thou shalt be at my side from this hour.
Bring me wealth and with blessing shower,
Let my prosperity from this time flower.

Now plant the seeds and visualize each seed becoming a beautiful flower, a symbol of prosperity and wealth. For best results, concentrate on a singular objective. For example, a substantial raise in pay, or if you are self-employed, visualize more clientele. The more precise you are in defining your goal, the better chance you have of reaching it. Next, put the talisman in the gold bag and keep it in your purse or wallet. As often as possible, take the talisman out of the bag and hold it. Use the Prosperity Chant to reinforce its power and purpose.

Once the flowers have blossomed, choose the nicest one and place it in the gold pouch along with the talisman. Choose the brightest and most colorful flowers for drying. These can then be used to enhance the properties of prosperity oil and incense. The remaining plants should be allowed to go to seed. The seeds can then be stored and used for future magickal works.

Personal Power Talisman Spell

Personal power is important, because it sustains self-confidence and moral fortitude. It also maintains your self-esteem and helps you bring into physical reality the things or events you most desire. Personal power is your divine spark and motivation. It gives you peace of mind and keeps you from being a victim.

To make this personal power talisman you will need the following items: the Personal Power Pentacle engraved on an iron disk or

Personal Power Pentacle

reproduced on red construction paper, a small wood box painted red, Mars oil and Mars incense,[7] charcoal, one red candle, five small garnets, a red ribbon, parchment paper, and a red ink pen.

The best time to make this talisman is on a Tuesday during the new moon. Center and ground yourself. Light the charcoal and place some incense on it. On the parchment paper, write your name and the following words with the red ink pen:

I now have the power to be, and do all that I desire.

Place some more incense on the coals. Open the red box and place the parchment paper in it, the personal power talisman, and the five garnets. Close the box and set it aside. Dress the red candle with the Mars oil as you chant the following:

Glory of Mars, pulsing bright
Bring me power, strength, and might.

Place the candle on top of the box and allow it to burn completely out. If there is any wax left, put it in the box. Tie the box up with the red ribbon and place it near your bed or under your pillow. The energy of the talisman will reinforce the concept of personal power as you sleep.

Love-Drawing Talisman Spell

This love drawing talisman enlists the power of Venus, the Roman goddess of love, beauty, and courtesans. Venus represents the personification of beautiful, uninhibited, and overwhelming love. Venus was, and still is, considered to be the essence of feminine beauty and desire.

---

[7]To make Mars oil, mix five drops each of the following essential oils: allspice, galangal, ginger, pennyroyal, and pine. To make Mars incense: mix equal amounts of ground allspice, dragon's blood, deer's-tongue, and galangal. Add five drops of Mars oil.

Items needed: one green silk pouch, the Second Pentacle of Venus engraved on a copper disk or drawn on green construction paper, one green candle, Venus incense and Venus oil,[8] charcoal for incense, seven small emeralds, seven pink rose petals, a needle, and green embroidery thread.

Second Pentacle of Venus

Perform this spell on a Friday during the waxing moon. Take the green pouch and sew the symbol for Venus (♀) on both the front and back, using the green thread. Put the rose petals and the emeralds in the bag. Set the bag aside.

Dress the green candle with the Venus oil and light it. Put a pinch of the Venus incense on the charcoal. When the incense begins to smolder, pass the Venus pentacle through the smoke, and then through the flame of the candle. As you do this, chant the following seven times:

> *Pentacle of Air, pentacle of Fire*
> *Filled now with my desire,*
> *Bring me love, bring me passion*
> *As this talisman I now fashion.*

Put the pentacle in the bag, then place the bag next to the green candle. When the candle has completely burned out, put the talisman in your purse or pocket and carry it with you.

---

[8]To make Venus incense, mix equal parts of ground orris root, benzoin, and sandalwood. Add seven drops of Venus oil. To make Venus oil, mix equal parts of the essential oils lilac, orchid, peach, rose, sweet pea, violet, and one drop of cherry oil.

Saturn Protection Talisman Spell

This spell is to help protect as well as return all negative thoughts and vibrations which are sent your way. Saturn is considered to be formation and the first law of karma (limitation). It is the planet's ability to limit which makes it a powerful influence in protection spells.

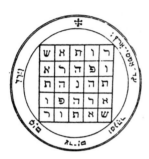

Saturn Pentacle

Items needed: one black candle, one mirror, and two Saturn Pentacles inscribed on white parchment paper with black ink. Make one large pentacle the same size as the mirror, and a smaller one to carry with you at all times.

Glue the large Saturn Pentacle to the back side of the mirror with its inscribed side facing out. Take the mirror and place it so the reflective side faces the direction from which negativity is coming. This will be the direction in which the person who is sending you the negative energy lives. Take the black candle and hold it firmly in your right hand as you focus your attention. When you feel ready, chant the following:

> *Candle black, Saturn's power*
> *Reflect back from this hour*
> *Negative thoughts sent to me.*
> *As I will, so mote it be!*

Now light the candle. Place the candle on top of the small pentacle in back of the mirror. Visualize all the negative thoughts and vibrations being reflected back to their place of origin. Feel the black candle absorb and consume any negative residue which may be in the room. Allow the candle to burn for one hour and then extinguish it. Repeat this procedure for three consecutive nights. On the last night, allow the candle to burn out. Leave the mirror in place and carry the small pentacle with you at all times.

Amulets

The amulet is an object that has been left in its virgin state and is then psychically charged or energized with a specific purpose in mind. Amulets are usually used for protection, since they are passive in their communicative abilities. Only when their barriers have been crossed do they react or retaliate. A good example would be the horseshoe over the door, which brings luck to all who cross beneath it; another example is the Udjat Eye, an Egyptian amulet which is supposed to bestow invulnerability and eternal fertility.

Almost any symbolic object can be turned into an amulet. Special stones, shells with markings, wood carvings, or statues— anything which already exists or is in a natural state can be turned into an amulet simply by forcing your will and dynamic energy into it. Because of its passive nature, and the fact that most of the amulet's power resides in its intrinsic symbolism, there is no need for formal consecration.

Selected Amulets

The Scarab: This is a replica of the Egyptian dung beetle. It is usually made from stone or clay. The beetle *(Scarabaeus sacer)* was the symbol of the sun god Khepera, a self-created and self-sustaining force. Khepera, the "roller" of the sunball across the sky, was likened to the beetle

The Scarab

rolling a dung ball containing its eggs along the hot stretch of sand. To the Egyptian mind, the teeming life bursting forth from the dung ball as the insects hatched represented the fertility of the land engendered by the sun's passage. In time, the scarab beetle came to be the hieroglyph for "existence" and an amulet signifying life and rebirth.

The Ankh: The ankh is a symbol which stands for everlasting life, as well as regeneration. Almost every Egyptian god is seen at sometime carrying or holding an ankh. The ankh amulet was made from wood, metal, gemstone, or faience. The ankh gave to its wearer the capacity to live life to the fullest degree. As the symbol of regeneration, the ankh can be worn for success as well as for protection.

The Ankh

The Udjat, or Eye of Ra, or Eye of Horus: The eye may face left or right; this does not matter, as it is still a form of protection and good health. Because of its association with Ra (the high god of Egypt), the *udjat* was considered to be a potent amulet which would bring strength, vigor, and soundness to its wearer. Like the scarab and the ankh, the *udjat* was usually made from a variety of materials, such as gold, silver, copper, wax, wood, or gemstone.

The Udjat

The Hecate Wheel: The symbol of the goddess of the crossroads and emblem of the eternity of Witchcraft. It can be used for protection or to help in invoking the Goddess herself. This is usually imprinted on a small round disk of silver, wood, or

The Hecate Wheel

ceramic, and is worn on a cord around the neck or carried in a pouch.

The Pentacle: The symbol of the spirit in control of the forces of nature or the elements of ordinary life. This is usually made of silver, gold, pewter, or other metals, and is worn around the neck for protection from negative vibrations. (This can be consecrated into a talisman or just worn as a protective amulet or luck charm.)

The Pentacle

The Conjure Bag: This can be made as an amulet or charm to give to a friend or turned into a talisman for yourself through the consecration ritual. For this you will need a red cloth bag into which you place the following items:*

1 Lodestone
1 High John root
1 Rusty nail
7 Job's tears
1 Devil's shoestring root
3 Pinches dragon's blood resin
7 Pinches lavender
1 Whole nutmeg from India
1 Red feather
1 Black feather
1 Clear quartz crystal
1 Bloodstone
1 Object belonging to the person the bag is for

The Conjure Bag

*All of these items may be purchased through any good mail order occult supply house. Most New Age book stores, and even some health food stores, now carry crystals, herbs, incense, oils, and a variety of magickal objects. If you live in an area without these resources, you can order your supplies from the list given in Chapter 12 of this book.

TALISMAN CORRESPONDENCE CHART

Intent	Color	Metal	Stone	Oil
Finance	Green, Gold	Gold, Silver	Emerald, Jade, Topaz	Almond, Orange, Bayberry
Healing	Red, Green, Black	Iron, Copper, Lead	Bloodstone, Hematite	Eucalyptus, Rosemary, Lotus
Harmony	Pink, Blue, White	Silver, Copper, Tin	Kunzite, Aquamarine	Gardenia, Tuberose, Benzoin
Love	Pink, Red, Green	Copper, Silver	Pink Tourmaline, Emerald	Rose, Orris, Jasmine, Cherry
Prosperity	Yellow, Green	Silver, Gold, Copper	Topaz, Tiger's-eye, Citrine	Honeysuckle, Cinnamon
Protection	Black, Red, White	Lead, Iron, Silver	Onyx, Ruby, Crystal Quartz	Patchouly, Myrrh, Rosemary
Power	Red, Black, Purple	Iron, Lead, Gold	Ruby, Amethyst, Opal	Carnation, Cedar, Sandalwood
Success	Yellow, Orange	Mercury, Gold, Tin	Topaz, Sunstone, Amber	Allspice, Anise, Verbena

Thoughts and Ideas

Amulets, charms, and talismans play an important role in Witchcraft. In essence, they are the physical representations of a desire, or the motivation behind the magickal act. They are repositories of energy, which combine with human energy to create powerful psychic barriers, or force fields. These force fields affect everything which crosses their paths or which they come in contact with.

By virtue of their structure, talismans reinforce faith and the belief in an ideal or goal, and we all know that faith plays an important role in magick. If you believe that a talisman has power, then you automatically project the appropriate message. If you create a protection talisman, then you will feel protected and radiate self-confidence and courage. If you are looking for love, an appropriately designed talisman will help you transmit messages which will attract a desirable mate.

The most effective talismans are those that you make yourself. A store-bought talisman may have a certain amount of residual energy, but nothing compared to what you can devise. No one has the intense interest or concern for your welfare that you do. Because of this, anything you make will be more appropriately suited to manifesting your desire or helping you attain a specific goal.

15

An Occult Primer

To the man or woman dissatisfied with the conventional explanations of a philosophy and a science limited to the evidence of the five physical senses, occultism opens a rich vein of ore to be had for the working.

—Dion Fortune, *Sane Occultism*

The purpose of this final chapter is to present an overview of additional information not covered earlier in the book. Although some of the concepts considered are not necessarily associated with Witchcraft, they are nevertheless valuable to the magickally inclined. However, with the increasing popularity of New Age thought, more and more of the mystical arts, formerly considered the realm of the magician, are being assimilated into Witchcraft. Because of this, Witchcraft has seen a tremendous surge of growth and interest in the last few years. It is no longer treated as a superstitious custom of the ignorant, but rather as the craft of the scholarly.

The Astral Plane and How to Project

The Astral Plane is the working ground of the magician where the truth about all things is revealed. It is the place of angels, demons, fairies, and host to the elemental forces of nature. To the Witch and magician alike, the Astral Plane holds the secret of power and the key to the creation of miraculous effects on the physical plane.

The Astral Plane has often been defined as the realm of visual imagination, a celestial realm where all things are possible. As a result of its ethereal atmosphere, the Astral Plane remains a great mystery to most. For the fearless explorer, however, the Astral Plane is nothing more than uncharted land awaiting discovery.

The Astral Plane is just as real to the astral body as the material plane is to the physical body. To the traveler on the astral plane, the scenery and everything connected with it seems as solid as the most solid material appears to the physical eye. One may travel from one region of the astral to another simply by an act of will without ever moving his or her physical body.

When consciousness operates outside of the body, it takes the mind with it. However, rarely is the mind fully conscious. This is why, although over 90 percent of us project, seldom do we remember our experiences. Usually they are forgotten or passed off as vivid dreams.

Most Witches and magicians agree that there is no definite division between the world of matter and the world of the spirit. Rather, there are five intermediate dimensions between the two, each one just a little more spiritual and nonmaterial than the previous.

In effect, there are seven different planes. Your consciousness has the ability to explore five of these planes during an astral journey.

Body	Plane	Characteristics	Function
Physical	Physical	World of Matter	Biological
Etheric	Etheric	Intermediate	Magnetic
Astral	Astral	World of Emotions	Emotional
Mental	Mental	World of Thought	Thinking
Spirit	Spiritual	Pure Spirit World	Spirit

Astral Projection

There are several things which can cause or induce an astral journey without a lot of exertion or deliberate effort.

Suppressed Desire: A suppressed desire is one of the most potent forms of suggestion. Desires that cannot be fulfilled will often grow to such staggering proportions that a person will do literally anything to gratify them.

When the mind becomes possessed by a strong desire to accomplish or gratify something and the physical body is incapable of doing this, the desire may become so intense that the subconscious will try to fulfill it in the etheric world, via an astral projection.

Direct Suggestion: There is a saying that if you tell a fictitious story long enough and with enough fervor, even you will begin to believe it. In fact, if your power of imagination and ability to convince yourself is great enough, you can really get yourself to believe practically anything. This is the basic principle of positive thinking. Your subconscious can be reached in a very similar manner.

If you can imagine yourself astrally projecting hard enough, this suggestion will result in the induction of a conscious projection. With regard to astral projection, the types of imagined suggestions which can be used are:

- Visual Suggestion: This involves seeing yourself projected astrally onto a higher plane of existence.

- Symbolic Suggestion: This involves visualizing an exit point for the astral body, such as a tiny hole or tunnel, and projecting your consciousness through it.

- Sensation Suggestion: This involves actually feeling yourself projecting, or imagining, the sensations of projection.

A combination of any or all these imagination techniques can be used for astral projection or the externalizing of consciousness in a controlled manner.

How to Project

Start by selecting a peaceful place and time of the day when you will not be disturbed. Although this exercise can be done in a chair, it is best to lie flat on your back on a firm, but not hard, surface. Next, stretch yourself out and loosen your clothing. Relax. Begin by using the "relaxation exercise" in Chapter 2. As you direct your breathing, exclude all thoughts and sensations and fix your consciousness totally on the breathing process.

Make a conscious effort to go completely limp. Begin with your feet and, working upward, relax all of the muscles in your body. This should take about four or five minutes.

While in this relaxed state, visualize your inner self becoming very light and lifting free of your physical body. Imagine yourself floating directly above your body as though you were on a cloud of air. Allow yourself to experience this feeling for about five minutes and then slowly lower yourself (astral self) back into your body. Do this exercise several times until you feel comfortable floating, and then continue with the next step.

Once you feel that you are free of your body, walk into another room. Go slow and take the time to examine everything in it. Make note of pictures, how furniture is arranged, and where objects of interest are. Do this exercise several times, and then have someone rearrange the room just prior to your journey. After you have returned to your body, write down exactly what you saw and where everything was positioned. Return to the room and check on your accuracy. The results will then indicate if you actually did astrally project.

The Aura and How to See It

The aura is light and energy, the vibrant membrane that both joins and separates the subtle essence of all living things. Every living person, place, and thing has an aura which surrounds it. The aura transmits knowledge of its owner's personality to all who come within range. This subtle body of pulsing energy is what attracts or repulses physical contact.

Each and every thing in the universe wears its own distinctive pattern of colors by which its true condition may be read. To those who are sensitive enough to see an aura, it usually appears as an outer layer of constantly oscillating colors, punctuated by sudden flares or flashes which change according to emotion. With a rush of affection there will be flashes of rose pink; should the temper flare, the rose color will turn red; with illness or fear, all red turns ghost grey. These flashes usually appear on or near the chakras or acupuncture points (see page ___).

It is believed that the aura is a prephysical body which serves as a buffer zone between cosmic energies and the physical body. Basically, it protects the physical body from celestial fallout and psychic debris. The aura is such a potent part of physical structure that gifted psychics and healers are able to read it, and can often diagnose a disease long before serious symptoms manifest themselves.

How to See Your Aura

Sit before a large mirror in a dimly lit room; relax and let all unwanted energies go. Let your peripheral gaze rest in the area between your image and its background in the mirror. It is out of this no-space where nothing is that the aura appears. First, you will see a darkening of your outline as though your physical boundary

The Aura: The shaded area is where the aura usually appears.

is blurring and extending into the air around it. With patience you will begin to see a hazy replica of your outline "like waves rising from hot pavement." This wavering form is often seen as a kind of luminescence with a greenish tinge. This is your aura.

The Chakras and How to Clear Them

Chakras are energy and information centers located within the human body. They are often referred to as organs of psychic perception, etheric organs, or centers of psychic force. They are whirling vortexes of concentrated etheric energy, perceived clairvoyantly as colorful wheels or flowers, with glowing dense centers.

Each chakra is invisibly attached along the spine, from the base to the top of the head. It is believed that the major glands are plugged into the chakras so they can withdraw the "spirit" from the air. The essence of the spirit is then turned into a physical substance which flows through the bloodstream, distributing its energy throughout the physical body.

The Hindu yogas who regularly work with the chakras believe that the older the soul mind, the more "spirit" the chakra will assimilate. Each chakra vibrates at a different rate, giving it a distinct difference in pattern and color. The chakras are accessed and controlled through various systems of meditation and yoga.

The chakras serve as channels for spiritual or psychic information and energy. When one of the chakras becomes blocked it can sometimes cause a problem within the physical body. Should this happen, there are different yoga techniques and breathing patterns which will correct the situation.

The first chakra is called the Root Chakra, and is located at the base of the spine. It has a direct relationship to the ovaries and testes. The Root Chakra is aligned with the ability to survive. Therefore, all survival data and genetic information is located in this chakra.

The Root Chakra tells you what you need for survival as an individual. Problems in this chakra are likely to occur when you aren't grounded. This often occurs when you are trying to take care of another person's welfare and neglecting your own.

The second chakra is the Spleen Chakra, which is located three fingers below the navel, and has a direct relationship to the pancreas. This chakra governs the erotic world of sexuality, sensuality, and desire. It also has a direct impact on our emotions and how we feel toward other people.

Problems in this chakra are likely to occur when you are too open to the feelings of others. This can cause you to enter into a sympathetic state of complicity with them, and duplicate their emotions. When this happens you are acting off their data, not your own. Therefore, you need to learn how to distinguish between the emotions of others and your own.

The third chakra is the Solar Plexus Chakra and is located the solar plexus region, behind the navel. This chakra has a direct relationship to the adrenal gland and governs energy distribution. It disperses vital energy throughout the body and is your main control or power center. The Solar Plexus Chakra maintains energy balance.

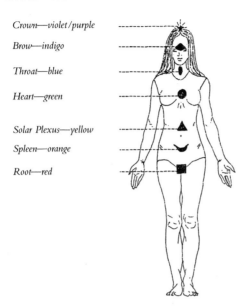

Crown—*violet/purple*

Brow—*indigo*

Throat—*blue*

Heart—*green*

Solar Plexus—*yellow*

Spleen—*orange*

Root—*red*

The Chakras

Problems can occur with this chakra when you constantly give in to the demands of avaricious people: the kind of folks who want your energy, money, property, and support with no strings attached. When you habitually give in to the demands of others, you deplete your energy reserves and sense of self.

The fourth chakra is the Heart Chakra. It is located at the sternum and has a direct relationship to the thymus gland. This chakra affects your ability to love, and to enter into a state of oneness, or self-love. This is the center of your nervous system, your universal life force. Your goals and life purpose develop in your fourth chakra. It is the meeting ground between your spiritual self and physical body.

Problems in this chakra occur when you are out of affinity with your higher self. If you cannot look at yourself with love, you cannot give or receive love.

The fifth chakra, or Throat Chakra, is located at the cleft of the throat and is connected to the thyroid gland. This is the chakra of communication, the vehicle through which you communicate to others. It provides the ability to express what you think and feel and is the communication point between your personality and your soul.

Problems occur in the fifth chakra when your communication with others is not clear, direct, and honest. We all communicate and grow through our words and emotional expressions. Let go of unfinished conversations, unspoken thoughts, and try to focus on the present.

The Brow, or sixth, Chakra is located between the eyebrows and is connected to the pituitary gland. This is considered your "third eye," the center of the individual spiritual consciousness. It has to do with clairvoyance and the ability to see auras and energy levels. This chakra provides the ability to arrive at a concept without going through rational processes; it is abstract intuition.

Through this chakra, individual consciousness is expanded into Universal Consciousness and allowed to merge with the Universal Mind. Problems with this chakra occur in two ways: the first is when people want you to see the world their way, which is considered social conditioning. The second way is when people plug into your personal consciousness and try to see where you are, thereby forcing validation. It is the "I want you to see me the way I want you to see you." This creates an enormous amount of personal tension. It is best to clear your life of people who are incapable of recognizing your individuality.

The seventh chakra is called the Crown Chakra and is located at the top of the head. (It is the soft spot on a baby's head.) This concerns knowingness, the ability to sit still, and know. It is the controller of all the other chakras, the center of cosmic awareness and spirituality. It is supreme consciousness, eternal peace, eternal knowledge, and what passes with you at death. This chakra connects humans with the infinite.

Problems in the seventh chakra come from people trying to own or manipulate you. Such situations block communications between you and your higher self. Don't allow others to manipulate you into a situation where you feel incompetent and without a thought of your own.

Chakra-Clearing Therapy

Sit quietly and relax, as in your general meditation exercise. Breathe in to a count of five and then exhale to a count of five. Do this several times, until you are completely relaxed.

Focus your consciousness on your Root Chakra. Continue your rhythmic breathing. Now breathe in and out from the Root Chakra. Visualize the area glowing red as you breathe.

Take a moment and rest, but continue with rhythmic breathing. Move your attention up to your Spleen Chakra. Breathe in and out through this chakra as you now visualize it glowing bright orange.

Rest and then continue. Move your attention up to your Solar Plexus Chakra. Breathe in and out through this chakra as you visualize it glowing bright yellow.

Rest and then continue. Move your attention up to your Heart Chakra. Breathe in and out through it as you visualize it glowing bright green.

Rest and then slowly move on. Breathe in and out through your Throat Chakra as you visualize it glowing turquoise blue.

Rest, continue breathing, and proceed to the Brow Chakra. Breathe in and out through the Brow Chakra and visualize it glowing bright blue.

Take a moment to rest, make sure your breathing is controlled, and then continue. Relax and force all of the energy you have gathered, working up the ladder of your chakras, out through the top of your head (your Crown Chakra) in a stream of violet light. Feel the energy flowing out and away from you, taking any negative or unclean energies with it. When you feel all the energy has stopped flowing, visualize the Crown Chakra close. Take a few moments to relax and then stand up. Position your hands over the top of your head and slowly move them down, palms inward, as you close each of the other chakras. Complete the exercise by taking a shower or bath to physically rinse away any leftover negative energies.

The Magic of Mirrors and How to Use Them

All mirrors are magickal because they signify truth, self-knowledge, wisdom, and the soul. They are considered to be a reflection of the supernatural, divine intelligence, and the ability to create. Because of its clarity, the mirror is a sun symbol, and as an indirect source of light, also a moon symbol. It symbolizes the mind of the sage and the ability to look into one's own nature. Magickally, mirrors can be used to divine the future or create a barrier of protection against psychic attack.

The art of divining the future by gazing into a mirror appears throughout the history of Western mysticism. A devotee of the goddess Demeter gazed into a sacred spring and predicted the harvest. It is believed that Catherine de Medici, a reputed Witch, depended on mirror divination to guide her through the tangled affairs of state in sixteenth-century France. And, the Grimorium Verum, published in 1517, includes directions for divining by the Mirror of Solomon.

Mirror Gazing

The most versatile mirror for augury is full-length with three panels. It provides a view of all three sides of an image at once, and when used with candlelight creates a very mystical effect.

To use the mirror for divining the future, the somber stillness of night is advised. Place the three-paneled mirror on a dresser or table in the corner of a darkened room. Before each panel, place a lighted candle. Position yourself so you can stare fixedly at the reflected image of the center candle flame. Ask your question and then look past the candle flame, deep into the mirror. Keep gazing into the mirror. The mirror will begin to cloud and fog as though it were covered by a veil of mist. Through the mist, an image will appear in answer to your query.

As the image begins to fade, the mirror will again begin to cloud and then will clear so that the candle's reflection is all that is left. Snuff out the candles and close the mirror. Be sure to record what you saw in your magickal journal or Book of Shadows.

Mirror Magick

There comes a time in everyone's life when protection is needed from outside negative forces. This is especially true for those involved in Witchcraft and the magickal arts. For some reason, it seems to be the delight of neophyte Witches to psychically attack their peers, solely for the sheer delight of doing it. In a case like this, where pristine ignorance is the motive, the offending individual warrants some obligatory time in the mirror box.

The mirror box is a reflective tool for turning one's own spitefulness against one's self. There is no need to thrust pins in a doll, invoke the demons of hell, or call upon the grim reaper, when a simple returning of negativity will suffice. Use common sense and think before you act. This doesn't mean you must turn the other cheek or become a living martyr, but rather be reasonable and don't join your rivals in the gutter.

Making and Using a Mirror Box

Items needed: one cigar box, or a medium-sized box with a lid, black construction paper or paint, mirror tiles,[1] a black candle, sandalwood oil and incense, and a picture of the person who brings you harm.

---

[1]Mirror tiles can be purchased in any hardware or building supply store.

Glue the construction paper to the outside of the box or paint it black. The idea is to create a black box. The next step is to cut the mirror tiles to size and glue them to the inside of the box. The reflective side of each mirror should be facing inward. This means that when you open the box you will be able to see your reflection.

Begin on a Thursday night, just before the moon turns new. Place the box on a table facing the direction where your enemy lives. Dress the candle with the sandalwood incense as you chant the following:

> *It is not to hate or burn,*
> *Just your evil to return.*

Now place the candle on top of the box and lean the picture up against it. Light the candle and some of the sandalwood incense. Stare at the picture and create a mental link with the individual as you chant the following:

> *For this hour I am the power.*
> *All that is evil and sent to me*
> *Is reflected back and returned to thee.*
> *This magickal box shall hold you tight*
> *As your wickedness turns against you this night.*
> *All that you have wished or sent to me*
> *Is now returned to you by law of three.*
> *As I now will, so it shall be.*

Open the box and place the picture inside. Close the lid and replace the candle on top of the box. Allow the candle to burn for one hour. Repeat this spell for three consecutive nights. On the third night (which should be Saturday, since you began this spell on a Thursday), seal the box shut by dripping some of the black candle wax on it. Allow the black candle to burn out and then place the box in the back of a closet or some other place where it will be safe from prying eyes. If the individual in the box should continue to vex you for some odd reason, repeat the spell.

The Pentagram, and the Lesser Pentagram Ritual

The pentagram is a five-pointed star. It represents the four elements (earth, air, fire, water) in subjection to the Akasha, or spirit. By all accounts, it is considered to be one of the most powerful protection amulets of the magickal arts. No self-respecting Witch or magician would ever leave home without one.

For centuries, ceremonial magicians have used the ritual of the pentagram as a prelude to their mystic rites. The ritual itself serves to cleanse the working area of negative vibrations. It can also be used to purge oneself of detrimental or obsessive thoughts. The nice thing about the pentagram ritual is it creates a positive atmosphere for working magick.

Begin the ritual with a short relaxing meditation to help clear your mind and body of stress and dissonant thoughts. When you feel the time is right, stand and face the east. Take your athame in your right hand and:

Touch your forehead and say: *Ateh* (thou art).
Touch your breast and say: *malkuth* (the kingdom)
Touch your right shoulder and say: *ve-geburah* (and the power)
Touch your left shoulder and say: *ve-gedulah* (and the glory).
Cross your hands over your breast and say: *le-olam (for ever)*.
Hold the athame up in front and say: *Amen.*

This then completes the Cabalistic Cross,[2] or opening of the ritual. Take several energizing breaths and continue with the actual inscribing of the pentagrams. Facing the East with your arm

[2]Cabalistic Cross: a ritual devised, in its modern form, by the Hermetic Order of the Golden Dawn.

outstretched, trace the pentagram with your athame. When the pentagram is complete, thrust your athame into the center of it and vibrate the deity name: Yod He Vau He.

Proceed to the South. Trace the invoking pentagram in the air with your athame, just as you did in the East. When the pentagram is complete, thrust your athame into the center of it and vibrate the deity name: Adonai.

Go to the West. Trace the invoking pentagram in the air with your athame. When the pentagram is complete, thrust your athame into the center of it and vibrate the deity name: Eheieh.

Move to the North. Trace the invoking pentagram in the air with your athame. When the pentagram is complete, thrust your athame into the center of it and vibrate the deity name: Agla.

Return to the East and complete the circle by thrusting your athame into the pentagram you first created. Now step back, and with arms outstretched so you form a cross, speak the following with great resolution:

> *Before me stands Raphael.*
> *Behind me stands Gabriel.*
> *At my right hand stands Michael.*
> *At my left hand stands Auriel.*
> *Before me flames the pentagram.*
> *Behind me shines the six-rayed star.*

Complete the ritual by repeating the Cabalistic Cross as you did in the beginning. The area is now ready for magickal work.

This ritual can be done as a self-protection rite as well. I know some people who do it every morning upon rising. The pentagrams act as a shield of protection throughout the day. The protective power of the rite does fade and dissipate with time, hence the reason it needs to be repeated at regular intervals.

The key to any ceremonial magickal act is visualization. You must be able to project a visual image of the thought-form you are working with so you can see and feel it. In this case, it would be the pentagram, a blazing star of energy and power, an arm's length away.

Closing Thoughts

The entire purpose of Witchcraft and magick is to create or cause a change. The key word here is *create*. In order for you to create or change something, you must take action. Desire is not enough unless it is followed through on both the material as well as the spiritual plane. Wishful thinking never changes anything, but action (work) does.

When all is said and done, Witchcraft is the most marvelous tool we have at our disposal. It permits us to create or reshape our own personal segment of the universe. When properly used, it allows us the freedom to become who and what we want. Witchcraft guides us along the path of spiritual renewal as it helps us express our highest aspirations. Nothing is impossible once the spirit has been aroused.

Glossary

Altar: a table used for magickal practice, usually placed in the center of the circle.

Amulet: an object left in its virgin state, psychically energized and used for protection against negative vibrations or to enhance one's psychic skills, usually worn as a charm.

Astral: (Latin: *astar,* for "star"): Refers to the level of awareness in the etheric world which is close to the mundane world.

Athame: the witch's double-edged knife, which is used to direct personal power during ritual.

Beltane: May Eve Sabbat, celebrated on April 30 in honor of the goddess of fertility. One of the eight sabbats.

Besom: the Witch's magickal broom.

Bind: to psychically constrict or restrain someone magickally to do your will.

Blessing: benediction; the laying on of hands to confer personal power, energy, or good will.

Boline: a white-handled knife used for cutting herbs and inscribing candles for magickal works.

Cakes and Wine: the ritual meal of bread or cakes, and wine.

Censer: an incense burner or heat-proof container for burning incense and magickal offerings.

Chakras: the seven major energy centers found on the human body.

Chalice: the Witch's magickal cup. A symbol of the Goddess. The chalice is used for blessing wine and other liquids during ritual acts.

Charm: Spoken words or a chant of magickal intent.

Circle: a sphere of magickal energy created by the Witch or magician. The circle is usually marked on the floor physically, and then charged by projecting psychic energy onto its boundary. The circle is a barrier for protection.

Conjuration: the act of summoning a spiritual force or energy source.

Conscious Mind: the place in the brain that manipulates information, environmental stimuli of hearing, seeing, tasting, smelling, feeling, and experiencing. Logical thought; the rational part of our consciousness.

Consecration: the act of blessing to remove or infuse an object with energy.

Coven: a group of Witches, usually led by a High Priestess and High Priest. Meets to celebrate the old gods and to work magick.

Craft: a term used in place of Witchcraft to denote magickal practice or Wiccan spirituality.

Deosil: to move in a clockwise direction.

Divination: the act of divining the future, fortune-telling, using symbols to foresee future events.

Divine Spark: minute specks of perfect light which are imbedded in every atom. The Divine Spark is that little speck of God everyone has.

Elemental: a deliberately formed and controlled thought-form of intelligent energy which is capable of performing menial tasks for its master.

Elements: the four building blocks of life which can be used to enhance magickal works: Air, Fire, Water, and Earth.

Energy: the vital activity which quickens inert matter which exists in all living, natural things and objects. The Witch experiences energy as the ability to project personal power.

Esbat: the Witch's weekly or fortnightly meeting. A meeting other than a sabbat.

Evocation: to summon or conjure an appearance of spiritual force.

Fascination: the process of casting a magickal spell upon someone using only the projection of personal power.

Glamour: fascination.

Grimoire: the Book of Shadows. A Witch's personal journal of magickal spells and rituals.

Hallows: Halloween, Samhain or Shamain, November Eve, October 31, the Festival of the Dead. One of the eight sabbats.

Handfasting: a Witch's wedding.

High Priest: initiated male leader of a coven.

High Priestess: initiated female leader of a coven.

Imbolc: the Feast of the Waxing Light celebrated on February 1; one of the eight sabbats.

Incantation: to sing and chant formulaic words, phrases, or sounds to raise energy for manipulation during spell-casting and ritual magick.

Initiation: the ritual process, or mystical ordeal, one goes through to symbolize the beginning of their spiritual life, and membership into a coven or group of like-minded people.

Invocation: (Latin: *invocatia,* for "to call upon"): The calling down or summoning of a God Force to aid the Witch or magician in their work. The act of invocation psychically links or binds the individual with the force to aid in the performance of psychic feats.

Lady: the title usually given to the High Priestess of a coven.

Linking: the process of using mental identification to communicate with spiritual forces, and/or with appropriate symbols in a magickal operation.

Litha: the Summer Solstice, the beginning of summer, around June 21; longest day of the year; one of the eight sabbats.

Lughnasadh: the first blessing of the harvest or bread made from the harvest, celebrated on August 1, one of the eight sabbats.

Mabon: the Autumn Equinox; beginning of fall, around September 21; celebrates the full bounty of the harvest; one of the eight sabbats.

Magick: comprises a system of concepts and methods of using the subtle forces of nature to help the individual alter reality. To cause change to occur in accordance with will.

Magnetism: magickal power, life force.

Magus: a male practitioner of magick, a wizard.

Meditation: a disciplined technique for prolonged concentration and personal reflection.

Mighty Ones: a term for the Guardians of the quadrants, archangels, or Divine Emanations.

Pagan: (Latin: *paganuas,* for "countryman"): a blanket word meaning a "heathen," or anyone who does not believe as I do, or is not a Christian, Jew, or Muslim.

Palmistry: the reading of the palm to divine one's past, present, and future.

Pentacle: (Greek: *pente,* for "five"): a talisman used for magickal operations, usually in the shape of a round disk and inscribed with a pentagram to create a powerful magickal effect.

Pentagram: a five-pointed star, the most powerful symbol of all ceremonial rites. Emblem of Man in control of the four elements of nature (Air, Fire, Water, Earth).

Poppet: a human-shaped doll or figure used as a substitute during ritual for the individual it represents.

Power Object: a psychic battery; an object which has been charged with power and energy to effect a certain result.

Psychic Awareness: the sensitivity of the body and mind to subtle vibrations usually emanating from the Astral Plane or from another human being.

Reincarnation: the process by which the life force does not die, but goes on living and in time is returned to life on earth.

Ritual: a prescribed event or a particular form or ceremony that is built up by tradition through repetitious activity.

Runes: ancient magickal script, the remnants of the old Teutonic alphabet, recently ascribed to small stones or tiles with the Teutonic alphabet figure etched on each stone or tile.

Sabbat: a Witch's religious festival celebrated eight times a year.

Samhain: See "Hallows."

Scry: to divine the future by gazing into a mirror or crystal ball.

Shade: the spirit of a dead person.

Sigil: a magickal seal usually comprised of a set of lines, numbers, or symbolic figures and usually inscribed on parchment.

Simple: a philter derived from a single herb.

Solitary: in witchcraft, this refers to someone who practices their magick, and religion, alone.

Spell: a period of time during which a person or object is held captive by a psychic force for the benefit of another person. Refers to folk magick and simple rites of a nonreligious nature.

Talisman: (Greek: *teleo*, for "to consecrate"): an inanimate object consecrated with psychic energy to serve its owner by creating changes in his or her environment.

Thurible: a censer, incense burner.

Visualization: the process of making thought-forms or forming mental images to enhance magickal work and spell-crafting. The ability to re-create an image once seen in the mind. Total recall.

Wand: one of the four major working tools of the Witch. It is symbolic of the air element, and is used for directing energy.

Wicca: a current and more popular name for Witchcraft. A neo-Pagan religion which expresses a reverence for nature, a polytheistic view of deity, and practices simple ceremonies to achieve communion with the natural forces of Mother Earth.

Widdershins: the term used for counterclockwise motion within a ritual circle.

Yule: the Winter Solstice, around December 21, celebrates the rebirth of the sun; one of the eight sabbats.

SPELL-CRAFTING AND SHADOW WORK

The following spells are ones that I have been teaching people for years. They are simple to perform and don't require impossible-to-find ingredients. In fact, most of the items used in the spells are readily available in your own home or can be purchased from any mail order house. For those who are so inclined, the recipes for some of the oils and incenses are included as footnotes.

The spells presented here are divided into four categories: love, friendship, success, and protection. Many of the spells have been designed for students and young adults facing adult problems for the first time. Each spell is complete, listing the ingredients, proper timing, and exact step-by-step instructions for its performance.

Be sure to read through the spell you will be doing several times. Don't forget to make your ritual checklist and organize all items needed prior to the work. And last but not least, you are the best judge of what you need and are able to maintain. If you doubt what you are doing or feel bad about it, then you have no business doing it. On the other hand, if it feels right and you are willing to accept responsibility for your actions, then go for it.

Spells to Attract Love

Since the beginning of time, men and women have sought ways of winning favor in the eyes of persons for whom they had an especially deep feeling or passion. In many cases, these people found that the great love that they had for a particular individual was not reciprocated. These, of course, were most painful and disappointing experiences. As most of us realize, at least those of us who have been subjected to the anguish of unrequited love, this type of rejection is exceptionally painful. When all the normal methods of winning the love of a certain person have been exhausted, many people look for some other means of gratifying their wish. This is where Witchcraft usually comes in. By utilizing a variety of spells and incantations, it is possible to procure a lover who might otherwise have remained unobtainable forever.

Warning: love spells work well to get someone's attention or to give a relationship a chance, *but it is unwise to use them to try to hold someone against their will.* When this is done, the only thing keeping the person with you is the energy of the spell. The first time you forget to do the spell, or aren't able to, its energy is gone and the relationship is over.

The Love Box

Items needed: a small heart-shaped box, love-drawing incense, love-drawing oil, a pink candle, parchment paper, a pen, rose quartz, some of your own hair, orris root powder, charcoal, and matches.

Perform this spell on the first Friday after the moon turns new. To prepare, center and ground yourself. Light the charcoal. Inscribe upon the parchment that which you specifically desire in a lover. Place some love-drawing incense on the coals. Dress the pink candle with love-drawing oil while saying:

> *May the Gods of love hear my plea*
> *And bring everlasting love to me!*

Light the candle and read your petition aloud, then place the candle on top of the parchment paper. Place more incense on the coals. Meditate upon your wish, and when finished, read the following:

Hail to thee, Goddess of Love
Shine down on me from above.
Bring now a lover to me.
As I will, so it shall be.

Let all items remain as they are until the candle has completely burned out. Place the parchment paper in the bottom of the box. On top of the paper, drip seven drops of the love-drawing oil. Next place your hair, the rose quartz, some of the orris root powder, and the candle drippings in the box. The box should then be placed where it will be most effective.

The Love Bottle Spell

Items needed: one large spice jar, painted pink and decorated with red ribbon and lace; one red candle; your birthstone; one teaspoon of basil; the love-drawing sigil (pictured below; trace or photocopy it right from this book).

The night before the full moon, take all of the above objects and go to a secluded spot. Light the red candle. As the wax drips, add the basil to it a little at a time. When the candle has been totally consumed and all of the basil has been added, shape the warm wax into a heart, saying:

Wax to heart, thou art transformed
Two become one, and love be warmed.

Before the wax cools completely, place the birthstone in the center of the heart. Place this in the jar on top of the sigil. The jar should now be consecrated with salt, water, incense, and fire. Then hold the jar in your power hand, placed against your heart, and say:

> *Elements and powers that be,*
> *Let love now come unto me.*
> *By the heart and by the stone,*
> *I'll no longer be alone.*
> *Come to me, come to me,*
> *As I will, so shall it be.*

Keep this jar in your bedroom. Whenever you go on a date or to a school dance, take the heart out of the bottle and carry it with you. If you plan to entertain a special guest or have a party, place the jar in the room where you will be entertaining.

The Rose and Ice Love Spell

Items needed: one small red candle, one red rose, a container to freeze the rose in, one large flat box filled with sand placed on the floor in front of your altar.

Several hours before you begin this spell, freeze the rose in the container filled with water. When it is frozen solid, take the iced rose to your ritual area. Place it on your altar and light the red candle. Next, draw the symbols below into the sand.

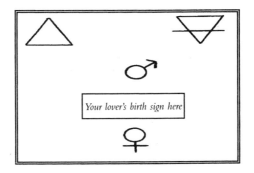

Put the frozen rose in the middle of the symbols over your lover's sign, set the burning candle next to the rose, and leave the area. When you return several hours later, the ice will have melted and so will your lover's heart. The only thing that is left is the rose, which symbolizes the flowering of eternal love. Pick up the rose and hold it next to your heart as you visualize your lover's smiling face and feel his (or her) loving embrace.

Golden Candle Enchantment Spell

Items needed: one gold candle, self-hardening clay, some handwriting and hair belonging to your loved one.

Light the gold candle and fashion a doll in your likeness from the clay. In the region of the heart, place your lover's hair and handwriting as you do this, and chant the following with feeling and emotion:

> *Go where I go and do what I do,*
> *And I will follow in your steps.*
> *Be a part of me and guide my way.*
> *Likewise, I'll be part of you and guide your way.*
> *Together we will not give or take, but share.*
> *Alike—alike in our differences—forever.*

Take the clay image to the highest hill closest to your lover's home. Bury the image in the earth. Turn and walk away. Do not look back. Return home and let nature take its course.

A Spell to Procure a Lover

Items needed: one white altar candle, three small pink candles, one sheet of white parchment paper, red ink and pen, one bottle of rose oil, a large incense burner or heat-proof dish.

On the night of the full moon, prepare your magick circle and light the white altar candle in advance. In the center of the piece of white parchment paper, draw the following design:

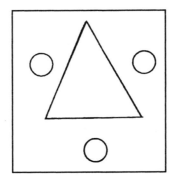

Inside the large triangle you should write, in longhand, a description of the type of person you wish to attract. If you already know the person, then write their name and how you wish them to feel toward you. Dress each one of the pink candles with the rose oil. Place the candles on the circles outside of the triangle and the rose oil in the center of the triangle. Light the candles. As the candles burn, visualize the one you desire.

When the candles have completely burned out, take the parchment paper with the inscription, light it in the flame of the white altar candle, and place it in the dish, allowing it to be consumed into ashes. As the paper burns, the following incantation should be chanted:

Hail blithe Eros, dear spirit of love;
Hail fair Venus in the realms above.
I ask a boon, a gift that is great,
Send me a lover with whose soul I shall mate.
In heavenly tone, prolonged and high,
Sweet Venus answers, her voice but a sigh.
As ashes of flame drift skyward to thee,
So will love fall gently downward to me.

Wear the rose oil as perfume to attract the one whose love you desire.

Love–Binding Spell

Items needed: two red cloth dolls made in the image of you and the one you desire. Fill each doll with the following herbs: foxglove, clove, orris root, blessed thistle, coriander, yarrow, and Solomon seal. Tag-locks of the couple to be bound, a twenty-one-inch piece of red cord, love-drawing oil, love-drawing incense and burner, a red candle and holder.

Begin on the Monday closest to the new moon and perform the spell for seven consecutive days, ending on a Sunday. Consecrate the elements and cast the magick witch's circle. Begin the spell by carving your name and your lover's on the red candle. Place some love-drawing incense on the coals. Dress the candle with the love-drawing oil as you chant the following:

> *Candle of love*
> *Work me this spell,*
> *That the one I do love*
> *Shall love me as well.*

Light the candle and place more incense on the coals. Take each doll and pass it through the incense, and then the candle flame, saying the following:

> *Air and Fire,*
> *Bring forth my desire.*

Place each doll seven inches away from the candle and then chant the following seven times:

> *I enchant you by Earth and Heaven,*
> *Turn to me, turn to me, turn to me*
> *By seven.*

Through moonlight and black of night,
All my love you shall requite.
Think of me and think of pleasure,
Turn to me in daily measure.
Turn to me, turn to me, turn to me.
As I will, so mote it be!

Repeat this spell for the next six days. Each time, move the dolls one-inch closer to the candle. On the last day, the dolls should touch the candle. At this time let the candle burn completely out. Bind the dolls together with the red cord and hide them in a place where both of you are sure to be or meet.

This spell works really well for couples who are engaged to be married. It helps bind them together during the waiting period and bring them peacefully through the chaos of wedding plans and preparations.

Ancient Gypsy Love Spell

This enchantment is best used to win the love of a man or woman who remains indifferent to your charms.

In a red vase or pot, plant a small sprig of ivy (the ivy carries the idea of constant, ever-growing, and reviving love). As the plant is watered, repeat this spell with your eyes closed:

As the ivy grows
And the leaf blows,
Let [lover's name] yearn to be
Ever constant unto me.

Thereafter, nurture the plant carefully, and nature will take its course. If the plant grows well, you will gain the love of the one you so desire. If the plant fails and dies, the love was not meant to be.

Spells to Win Friendship

Winning the acceptance and admiration of other human beings is a universal desire of all people. When a person has friends who really care, he or she is able to bear up under almost any ill fortune which may occur. For years, Witches have used their magic in times of despair and loneliness to find friends and bring happiness into their lives.

Circle of Friendship Spell

Items needed: one pink candle for each person you wish to befriend, and one gold candle to represent yourself; one sprig of rosemary and one of lavender.

Under the light of the new moon, inscribe a circle into the earth. Place the pink candles, evenly spaced, around the edge of the circle. In the center of the circle, lay the rosemary and lavender sprigs in a cross formation. Place the gold candle next to the center of the cross. Take a few moments to relax. Visualize yourself and the circle of friends having a wonderful time.

Light the gold candle first, and then in a clockwise direction light each of the pink candles. Chant the following once for each friendship candle:

> *As the stars above in darkness shine*
> *With a light that fills the heavens divine,*
> *So bright with radiance our friendship glows,*
> *Outshining the sun and dimming all foes.*

Allow the candles to burn for one hour and then extinguish them. Repeat the spell every evening until the candles have burned out. Save the rosemary and lavender, for future use in amulets and talismans.

Circle of Friendship Spell as a Group Work

Items needed: one pink candle for each person in the group; one gold candle to represent the group as a whole; one long sprig of rosemary and one of lavender.

Under the light of the new moon, one member of the group will inscribe a circle into the earth. Once the circle has been etched into the earth, each person in the group will carve their name into the gold candle. The last person to carve their name into the candle will light it and place it in the center of the circle along with the sprigs of rosemary and lavender.

In turn, each person will light their pink candle, come forward one at a time, and place it on the rim of the circle as they repeat the following:

> *As the stars above in darkness shine*
> *With a light that fills the heavens divine,*
> *So bright with radiance our friendship glows,*
> *Outshining the sun and dimming all foes.*

When all of the candles have been set in place, everyone will take hands to form a circle around the candles. In unison, the group will then intone the previous chant seven times. When the rite is completed, the candles should be extinguished. Each member will take their own candle and some of the rosemary and lavender with them.

A Friendship Box

In a ceramic box, place these items: pansies (for love), rosemary (for good will), pine needles (for steadfastness), a shiny penny (for honesty), a tiny sprig of violets (for kindness), and a gold ring (for unity). Include a personal item, one the recipient knows is meaningful to you. Close the box and bind it with green, white, and gold ribbon. Place the box on your friend's doorstep.

Lasting-Friendship Spell

Items needed: Four smooth stones painted with these symbols:

Red Oak Leaf   Green Lilac Sprig   White Snowflake   Gold Sun

In addition to the painted stones, you will need a picture of yourself and your friend, four candles, (red, autumn; white, winter; green, spring; and gold, summer). Inscribe your magick circle on the floor or in the earth. Arrange the stones and the candles in the following manner:

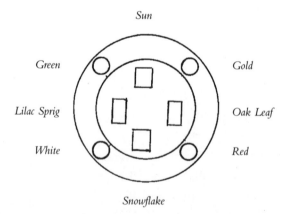

Cast your magick circle and light the candles. Take the picture of yourself and the one of your friend and seal them together with wax from each of the burning candles. To do this, take each of the four candles and tip them to the side, letting a drop of wax fall on each of the four corners of the photograph. Press the two pictures together, facing each other. Place the pictures in the center of the circle of stones. Take a moment and visualize you and your friend. When you feel the time is right, recite the following chant nine times:

> *Friendship is a gift the gods bestow,*
> *It lives through heat and rain and snow.*
> *With these candles I form the bond,*
> *That will endure this life and beyond.*

Allow the candles to burn out. Place the pictures and painted stones in a pink pouch. Store the pouch in a safe place.

Spells to Attract Money and Personal Success

Making ends meet in today's world is often a challenge. For many people, living expenses alone make it impossible to save money or invest for future security.

There is no reason for anyone to want. With a simple change of attitude, positive action, and a little magickal help, anyone can go from being a pauper to a prince. Money is not the root of all evil, but a lack of it can turn the most honest and hard-working individual into a real monster.

A word of advice: it is not a good idea to cast spells for money unless you have a seed to plant. In other words, nothing begets nothing. Casting a spell for money when you have none will only expand the situation. Most spells call for a certain amount of monetary investment to procure the items needed for working the spell. Money makes money, and most money spells work best when used to expand or enhance an already existing situation.

Asking for money when you don't even have a job is bound to fail. First do a spell to help get yourself a job. Once gainfully employed, you can then do a spell to increase and expand your weekly paycheck. By doing this, you are working with the natural flow of the universe, and will surely succeed.

Seven-Day Money Spell

Items needed: one (glass) seven-day green candle, several shiny new coins, money-drawing oil, one piece of virgin parchment paper, a green marking pen, a gold-painted bowl filled with water and large enough to hold the candle.

Begin this spell on the night of the new moon. Place all of the needed items on your altar and cast the magick circle. Remove the green candle from its glass container. On one side of the candle carve the amount of money you need, and on the other side of the candle carve your name. Dress the candle with the money-drawing oil as you chant the following:

> *Money, money come to me,*
> *This I will, so mote it be.*

Return the candle back to its glass container. Next, take the parchment paper and draw three large dollar signs with the green ink pen. As you draw the dollar signs, repeat the chant.

Put the seven-day candle into the bowl filled with water and place this in the center of your altar on top of the parchment paper. Light the candle and repeat the chant seven times. Carefully drop the coins into the bowl as you visualize the amount of money you need coming to you. Do not extinguish the candle; it must burn for a full seven days.

Each night when you come before your altar, kneel and drop several coins into the bowl. As you do this, repeat the chant seven times. On the last night, after the candle has been consumed, empty the water out of the bowl onto the earth. Place the coins in the empty glass. Place the glass next to your bed or desk, and continue to put coins in it. When the jar is filled, your wish will be granted.

Charm Bag for Money

Items needed: a one-dollar bill, sixteen cloves, two loadstones, one whole nutmeg, one High John the Conqueror, one green silk pouch, and your birthstone.

Place all of the necessary items into the silk pouch as you visualize large sums of money coming your way. In your mind's eye, see yourself getting that long-awaited pay raise or special bonus. If you play the lottery, take the bag to bed with you and ask for the winning numbers to appear in your dreams. If you are a student, visualize a part-time job, a bigger allowance, or a college grant. No matter what your desire, once the bag has been filled, tie it shut and charge it by saying:

> *The money I need is now within sight,*
> *I grow rich and prosperous from this night!*

Carry the bag with you at all times until you have the money you need.

High John Money Spell

Items needed: Seven green candles, one bottle of High John the Conqueror oil,[1] one packet of High John the Conqueror powder,[2] one whole High John the Conqueror root, and one jar of honey.

Begin this spell on a Thursday during the waxing moon. Place all the required items on your altar. Take one of the green candles and dress it with the High John oil. Next place the High John root into the jar of honey. Sprinkle some of the powder over the root in the jar. Put the lid on the jar and set the candle on top of it. Light the candle and chant the following seven times:

---

[1]High John the Conqueror oil can be purchased from any occult mail order supply house, or it can be made by placing a High John root into a small bottle of oil.

[2]High John the Conqueror powder can also be purchased from any occult mail order supply house, or it can be made by grinding a High John root with pure talcum powder.

Money come from far or near,
Stacks of money pile up here.
Will and words, sweet like honey
Bring me all kinds of money.

Allow the candle to completely burn out. Repeat the spell each day until all seven candles are gone. Take the jar of honey and bury it beneath an oak tree. Walk away and do not look back.

Attraction and Personal Success

Items needed: a yellow altar cloth, success incense, a yellow candle, attraction oil, the First Pentacle of the Sun, church charcoal.

First Pentacle of the Sun

This spell should be done on a Sunday morning during the waxing moon. Light the incense. In your mind's eye, see yourself being successful in all you do. Take the yellow candle and dress it with the attraction oil. As you do this, see clearly what you want coming to you. As you are rubbing the oil on the candle, chant the following:

Power of the rising sun,
Let success to me now come.

Light the candle and place some more incense upon the coal. Now take the Sun Pentacle and pass it through the candle flame and the incense smoke as you say the following six times:

This talisman shall bring to me
Honor, wealth, and prosperity

Place the talisman beneath the candle and chant the following, forcing all your energy into the candle and the talisman:

> *Success and prosperity come to me,*
> *For this I will, so mote it be!*

Allow the candle to burn for one hour. Repeat the spell for six days. On the sixth day, allow the candle to burn out, and carry the Sun Pentacle with you at all times. If you are a student, you can place the pentacle in a frequently used notebook or your backpack. For those in sales, place the pentacle in your sales or display case. Women on the go can always place the pentacle in their purses or a briefcase. The important thing is to keep the talisman with you as much as possible.

Treasure Map of Success

The treasure map is a physical prop which aids the creative visualization process. It is an outward symbol of an inner desire. By making such a map, you reinforce your destination, and thereby stay focused on its development.

Treasure maps come in all sizes and shapes. They can be made by anyone, young or old, and for a variety of purposes. Students will find the map helpful for completing projects and passing tests. Couples looking to purchase a home can treasure-map their financial strategy. Professional men and women will find the map an ideal way to get a promotion or even find a better job. The possibilities are endless. If you can imagine it, you can make it happen.

The treasure map is a powerful tool. It brings together all of the necessary conditions which make it possible for you to achieve your goal. However, you must work along with the map to maintain the physical momentum of your journey. The map can help you get a job, but it can't go to work for you.

Before you begin to chart your map, you should choose one goal and concentrate on it. Write a brief description of your goal. Reduce the description to one sentence. When using magick, you should always be precise about what you wish to achieve; you need to express your goal in as few words as possible. For example, if you were a student, graduation would be your goal. Your point of focus would be, "I study, I learn, I graduate with honor."

Creating Your Treasure Map

Items needed: one large piece of heavy construction paper or poster board; colored pens, pencils, scissors, glue, tape, a ruler, and magazines for pictures.

Begin your treasure-mapping by choosing a goal and setting a timeframe. Next, pick out a pattern to form the background of your map. This can be any shape which is appealing to you. The cross, a calendar grid, and a pentagram are good examples of basic patterns:

Once you have decided on your goal, timeframe, and background pattern, you will then need to compose a positive statement expressing your intent. A good example would be the one above, by a student working toward graduation. In this case, the calendar grid pattern would work best, because most schools structure their teaching in monthly increments. The goal here would be to study, learn, and graduate with honors on a specific date. The following statement would then reflect this positive affirmation:

I will study each day.
I will complete all assignments on time.
I will gain knowledge and graduate with honors.

Work with your map for at least fifteen minutes each day. Meditate and focus on your goal. Add drawings, pictures, and written affirmations to the map which lead toward your goal.

Each time you accomplish a portion of your goal, celebrate the occasion. Always record your progress on the map, because this will encourage you to continue with the work you are doing.

The treasure map helps you accomplish two things: first, the map reprograms your subconscious mind to act and achieve; second, it releases your positive goal-oriented thought-forms onto the Astral Plane every day. This reinforces your actions as you move toward your goal. The treasure map allows you to work on both the physical as well as Astral Plane at the same time. By doing this you create a powerful magickal circuit between yourself, your goal, and the forces of light, which hastens the manifestation process.

Protection and Jinx-Removing Spells

Do not be deceived into thinking that everyone who wears a pentacle will embrace you with perfect love and perfect trust. When it becomes known that you are knowledgeable in the craft, there will always be individuals who will want to flex their magickal prowess at your expense. These individuals are usually mean-spirited and ineffectual. They have no life, and the only time they feel alive is when they are causing harm or creating chaos. There is no kind and loving way to deal with these folks, so it is best to just return a good dose of their own medicine to them.

Black Candle and Mirror Spell

Items needed: three black candles, a triangle-shaped mirror,[3] tag-locks (refer to Chapter 1) belonging to the individual who is causing you harm or pain.

On the night of the dark moon, place the triangle-shaped mirror on your altar, reflective side up. In the center of the triangle,

---

[3]Mirror tiles sold in hardware stores work well for these kinds of spells. They are flat and can be easily cut.

place the tag-locks of the individual whom you are trying to protect yourself against. Place one black candle at each point of the triangle.

Take several deep breaths, relax, and focus your attention on the triangle. Visualize the individual who is causing you harm. Now light each one of the candles, separately. As you light each candle, chant the following three times:

Candle of black
Moon mirror power,
Reflect and protect
Me from this hour.

Allow the candles to burn for one hour. Repeat this spell every night until the full moon. On the night of the full moon, allow the candles to burn out. Tape the tag-locks to the reflective side of the mirror and bury it in the ground near the home of the one at odds with you.

To Stop Gossip

Items needed: one lamb's tongue, a red-and-black ribbon, salt, lime juice, a piece of parchment paper, plastic wrap.

On the piece of parchment paper, write the name of the person who is spreading the gossip. Make a slit in the center of the lamb's tongue. Place the parchment paper inside the slit in the tongue. Fill the slit with salt and lime juice. Wrap the tongue in the plastic wrap and bind it with the red-and-black ribbon. Hang the tongue over the front door or in a high place close to your house. The tongue will need to hang for nine days, so it must be placed somewhere safe and out of the reach of animals. At the end of the nine days, the gossip will stop. Once this happens, you can then dispose of the tongue. Repeat whenever needed.

Protection for the House

Items needed: a square of parchment paper and a black pen.

Print the following letters on the parchment paper with the black pen:

S	A	T	O	R
A	R	E	P	O
T	E	N	E	T
O	P	E	R	A
R	O	T	A	S

Beneath the protective inscription, write the following:

Health to this house
Protected from all evil
Happiness on the hearth
Love for all within

Place the paper beneath the doormat at the main entrance to your home.

The Witch's Protection Bottle

Items needed: one small jar; a small amount of the following items: broken glass, nails, thorns, steel wool, wormwood, thistle, nettles, vinegar, salt, your own urine, and one black candle.

This spell should be done at midnight during the waning moon. Cast your magick circle. Fill the bottle with all the items listed above and seal it tightly. With the middle finger of your right hand, draw a pentacle on the lid of the jar with the consecrated water. Place the black candle on the lid of the jar and light it. Chant the following over the candle:

Candle of black, and hexes old
Release the powers that you hold.
Reverse the flow of spells once cast,
Leave pain and sorrow in the past.

Let the candle burn out. Take the bottle and bury it in the earth close to your home. The Witch's protection bottle will protect you from those who wish you harm. In most cases, the bottle will form a shield of protection for about six months. When the spell begins to weaken, just repeat it by making a new bottle.

Recommended Reading

There is no such thing as a bad book. A book may be poorly written or not to your taste, but this does not make it bad. All books contribute in some way to our personal growth, even if the only thing we glean from them is what not to do.

When one enters the field of Witchcraft and magick, it is always best to consider as many viewpoints as possible before making judgments. I say this because it is difficult to determine what will or will not work, unless you have a thorough understanding of the subject. The following list of selected books offers a variety of opinions and perspectives which will help you grow and progress in your Witchcraft studies.

Ashcroft-Nowicki, Dolores. *The Ritual Magic Workbook*. London: Aquarian Press, 1986.

Beyerl, Paul. *Master Book of Herbalism*. Custer, Wash.: Phoenix Publishing, 1984.

Bias, Clifford. *Ritual Book of Magic*. York Beach, Me.: Samuel Weiser, 1982.

Buckland, Raymond. *Practical Color Magic*. St. Paul: Llewellyn Publications, 1983.

Cunningham, Scott. *The Complete Book of Incense, Oils, and Brews*. St. Paul: Llewellyn Publications, 1989.

————. *Earth, Air, Fire, and Water*. St. Paul: Llewellyn Publications, 1983.

Denning and Phillips. *Creative Visualization*. St. Paul: Llewellyn Publications, 1983.

Dunwich, Gerina. *Candlelight Spells*. Secaucus, N.J.: Citadel Press, 1988.

Farrar, Janet, and Farrar, Stewart. *Eight Sabbats for Witches.* London: Robert Hale, 1981.

———. *The Witches' God.* Custer, Wash.: Phoenix Publishing, 1989.

———. *The Witches' Goddess.* Custer, Wash.: Phoenix Publishing, 1987.

Farrar, Stewart. *What Witches Do.* New York: Coward, McCann, and Geoghgan, 1971.

Gardner, Gerald. *Witchcraft Today.* Secaucus, N.J.: Citadel Press, 1955.

Green, Marion. *The Elements of Natural Magic.* Ringwood, Victoria, Australia: Elements Books, 1992.

———. *A Witch Alone.* London: Aquarian Press, 1991.

Heisler, Roger. *Path to Power, It's All in Your Mind.* York Beach, Me.: Samuel Weiser, 1990.

Hunter, Jennifer. *Twenty-first-Century Wicca.* Secaucus, N.J.: Citadel Press, 1997.

Huson, Paul. *Mastering Witchcraft.* New York: Perigee/GP Putman's Sons, 1970.

Innes, King, and Powell. *Fate and Fortune.* New York: Crescent Books, 1989.

Katzeff, Paul. *Full Moons.* Secaucus, N.J.: Citadel Press, 1981.

Lady Sabrina. *Cauldron of Transformation.* St. Paul: Llewellyn Publications, 1996.

———. *Reclaiming the Power.* St. Paul: Llewellyn Publications, 1992.

Lewis, J. R., and Oliver, E. D. *Angels A to Z.* Detroit: Visible Ink Press, 1996.

Mathews, John. *The World Atlas of Divination.* London: Bulfinch Press, 1992.

Modrzyk, Stanley J. A. *Turning of the Wheel.* York Beach, Me.: Samuel Weiser, 1991.

Morrison, Sarah Lyddon. *The Modern Witches' Spellbook.* Secaucus, N.J.: Citadel Press, 1980.

Skelton, Robin. *The Practice of Witchcraft Today.* Secaucus, N.J.: Citadel Press, 1990.

Starhawk. *The Spiral Dance.* San Francisco: Harper and Row, 1979.

Valiente, Doreen. *Witchcraft for Tomorrow.* New York: St. Martin's Press, 1978.